KU-768-249

GOLFING ART

GOLFING ART
Edited by Phil Pilley

Foreword by Tony Jacklin

Stanley Paul
London Sydney Auckland Johannesburg

Stanley Paul & Co. Ltd

An imprint of Century Hutchinson Ltd
62–65 Chandos Place, London WC2N 4NW

Century Hutchinson Australia (Pty) Ltd
89–91 Albion Street, Surry Hills, NSW 2010

Century Hutchinson New Zealand Limited
PO Box 40-086, Glenfield, Auckland 10

Century Hutchinson South Africa (Pty) Ltd
PO Box 337, Bergvlei 2012, South Africa

First published 1988
© Phil Pilley 1988

Designed by Julian Holland

Set in Garamond Light ITC by
Tradespools Limited, Frome, Somerset

Printed and bound in Great Britain by
Butler and Tanner Ltd, Frome and London

British Library Cataloguing in Publication Data

Golfing art.
  1. Paintings. Special subjects. Golf
  I. Pilley, Phil
  758'.9796352

ISBN 0 09 171 480 X

Contents

Work	Approx. date	Artist	
Golfers on the Ice near Haarlem	1668	Adriaen van de Velde	10
The Kolven Player	1654	Rembrandt van Rijn	12
Child Playing Golf	1650	Bartholomeus van der Helst	14
St Andrews	—	Unknown artist	16
Golfers beneath Edinburgh Castle	1746/7	Paul Sandby, RA	18
Landscape with Golfers	—	Unknown artist	20
William St Clair of Roslin	1771/2	Sir George Chalmers	22
William Inglis on Leith Links	1787	David Allan	24
William Innes ('The Blackheath Golfer')	1790	Lemuel Francis Abbott, RA	26
John Taylor	1830	Sir John Watson Gordon, RA, PRSA	28
First Meeting of the North Berwick Golf Club	1833	Sir Francis Grant, PRA	30
Old Alick	1839	R. S. E. Gallon	32
Caddie Willie	1839	C. H. Robertson	34
The Golfers: A Grand Match over St Andrews Links	1847	Charles Lees, RSA	36
A Golf Match	1844	Charles Lees, RSA	38
Summer Evening at Musselburgh	1859	Charles Lees, RSA	38
Allan Robertson	mid c.19	Unknown artist	40
John Whyte-Melville	1874	Sir Francis Grant, PRA	42
Allan Robertson and Tom Morris	1889	Thomas Hodge	44
William Park, Senior	1888	John A. T. Bonnar	46
Old Daw	1888	Thomas Hodge	48
Young Tom's Last Match	1875	Francis Powell Hopkins	50
Match at Blackheath, 1869	1869	Frederick Gilbert	52
Golf at Blackheath, 1875	1875	Francis Powell Hopkins	54
The Tee Shot	1877	Francis Powell Hopkins	56
Ladies' Match at Westward Ho!	1880	Francis Powell Hopkins	58
A Hazard on the Ladies' Course	1890	Lucien Davis, RI	60
Golf at St Andrews	1892	W. G. Stevenson, RSA	62
Dr Laidlaw Purves Playing at Wimbledon	1892	William E. Pimm	64
Dr W. Laidlaw Purves	1896	The Hon. John Collier	66
Members of Royal St George's, 1892	1892/3	Allen C. Sealy and C. Spencelayh	68
The First Club on the Continent	1893	Allen C. Sealy	70
Medal Day at St Andrews, 1894	1894	Unknown artist	72
The First Amateur Championship in America	1931	Everett Henry	74
John Ball, Junior	1899	R. E. Morrison, RCA	76
Match at Duddingston, 1898	1898	J. Michael Brown	78
Ladies' Championship at Aberdovey, 1901	1901	J. Michael Brown	80
Mixed Foursome	1900	A. I. Keller	82
Frederick Guthrie Tait	1901	J. H. Lorimer, RSA	84
Old Tom Morris	1903	Sir George Reid, PRSA, HRSW	86
Harold Hilton	1913	Richard Jack, RA, RI, RP	88
The Triumvirate	1913	Clement Flower	90
A Caddie to the Royal and Ancient	1914	W. Dendy Sadler	92
Lloyd George at Walton Heath	1916	J. Michael Brown	94
The Prince of Wales	1927	Sir William Orpen, RA	96
Nancy, Lady Astor at North Berwick	1924	Sir John Lavery, RA, RSA, RHA	98
Walter Hagen	1958	Frank C. Bensing	100
Bobby Jones	1930	J. A. A. Berrie, RCA	102
Henry Cotton	1938	J. A. A. Berrie, RCA	104
Golf at East Brighton	1940	Conrad Leigh	106
Ben Hogan	1967	J. Anthony Wills	108
Brancaster	1970	Julian Barrow	110
Gleneagles	1979	Arthur Weaver	112
The 18th at Pebble Beach	1983	LeRoy Neiman	114
12th Green, Augusta National	1985	Arthur Weaver	116
The Ailsa Course, Turnberry	1985	Kenneth Reed, FRSA	118
The Seventeenth	1985	William Binnie, DA	120
The Caricaturists			122
The Cartoonists, The Advertisers			124

Acknowledgements

The editor wishes to thank all those museums, galleries, golf clubs, other institutions, private owners and artists for their help in facilitating photography and/or making available for reproduction works owned or held by them. Particular thanks go to The Royal & Ancient Golf Club of St Andrews, Fife, Scotland (pages 16, 40, 42, 46, 48, 72, 84, 86, 90, 96, 104), the United States Golf Association, Far Hills, New Jersey (pages 20, 74, 100, 108), and Angus Lloyd of Burlington Galleries, 12 Burlington Gardens, London W1 (pages 50, 56, 64, 106, 110, 112).

Thanks in this respect are also offered to the following: Eduardo Alessandro Publications, Broughty Ferry, Dundee (120); © The Estate of H. M. Bateman, 1988 (124, lower right); BBC Hulton Picture Library (22); Courtesy of The Trustees of the British Museum (12, 18); Ian Dunlop (98); The Edward James Foundation (14); The Honourable Company of Edinburgh Golfers (28, 38 bottom); Harry Langton (44); ©LeRoy Neiman, Inc, courtesy Knoedler Publishing, Inc. (114); The Life Association of Scotland Group (78, 80, 94); The Medici Society (30); National Gallery of Scotland (24).

The National Gallery, London (10); Robert Opie Collection (125, CWS and Guinness ads.); Pau GC (70); Robert J. Perham (116); *Punch* Magazine (124, left); Felix Rosenstiel's Widow & Son, Ltd (124, 125, Lawson Woods); Royal Blackheath GC (26, 32, 34, 54); The Royal Company of Archers (22); Royal Liverpool GC (76, 88, 102); The Royal St George's GC (66, 68); Scottish National Portrait Gallery (30, 36); David I. Stirk (58); Tee-Mark, Ltd (118); John Walker and Sons Ltd (125).

Space regrettably makes it impossible for the editor to list all the hundreds of individuals who freely gave of their time to assist the compilation and content of this book, but perhaps he may be allowed to express his thanks to all concerned and to make particular mention of the following. They include the only person whose patience my checking for accuracy finally exhausted, but exclude the lady whose solicitors requested me not to contact her to check facts about the painting she owns and the man who declined to verify further information because I was not a member of his club!

Alistair Adamson; J. P. Audis (Sec/manager, Royal Burgess Society of Edinburgh); Archie Baird; Col H. F. O. Bewsher (Sec, Royal Company of Archers); John Bissell (Sec, Royal Blackheath Golf Club); Members of the British Golf Collectors Society; Bobby Burnet (Historian, R & A); Reg Chiswell (LAS Group); Charles Cruikshank (Royal Wimbledon GC); John Davidson (Sec, Royal Liverpool GC); John Davies (Sec, Royal N. Devon GC); Ray F. Davis (Curator, PGA/World Golf Hall of Fame, USA); Tim Dolby; Charles Dufner (*Golfiana*, USA); Sandy Heron (Sec, Walton Heath GC); Eric Heyden (Knoedler Publishing, Inc, USA).

R. J. Hitchen (Sec, Royal St George's GC): Harry Langton (who is currently planning a book on Thomas Hodge); Angus Lloyd; A. J. Macdonald (Langley Park GC); Dr R. Marshall and Mrs S. Kerr (Scottish National Portrait Gallery); David Martin (Minchinhampton GC); David Moody (Lothian District Librarian); Morton W. Olman (co-author of *Encyclopedia of Golf Collectibles*, USA).

Phaidon Press; Nick Potter (Burlington Galleries); John Richards; Janet Seagle (Curator, USGA); Duncan Smith (British Museum Prints and Drawings Dept); David I. Stirk (whose recent books have been a major contribution to golf history); Major J. G. Vanreenan (Sec, Hon. Co. of Edinburgh Golfers); Diana Willis; and Don Wood, who, with my son Kevin Pilley, helped me hugely in research. Also Renton Laidlaw who, with Ian Dunlop and Nick Potter, read the proofs.

Special Photography:
Peter Adamson, AIPP, St Andrews, Fife; Sheldan C. Collins, Weehawken, New Jersey 07087, USA; Richard Davies; Jack McKenzie, AIC Photography, Edinburgh; Roger T. Quayle, ABIPP 'Elsams', Liverpool; Geoffrey White, AIBP, ARPS, Addington Surrey.

Abbreviations
BWS = British Watercolour Society; DA = Diploma in Art; *exh.* = exhibited; *fl.* = flourished; H = Honorary; F = Fellow; LGU = Ladies' Golf Union; PRA = President of Royal Academy; PRSA = President of Royal Scottish Academy; R & A = Royal & Ancient Golf Club of St Andrews; RA = Royal Academy, Royal Academician; RBA = Member of Royal Society of British Artists, Suffolk St (SS); RBSA = Member of Royal Birmingham Society of Artists; RCA = Member of Royal Cambrian Academy, Manchester, or if artist *studied* at RCA, Royal College of Art, London; RHA = Member of Royal Hibernian Academy, Dublin; RI = Member of Royal Institute of Painters in Watercolours; RMS = Royal Society of Miniature Painters; RP = Royal Society of Portrait Painters; RSA = Royal Scottish Academy, Member of the RSA; RSW = Member of Royal Scottish Watercolour Society; RWS = Member of Royal Watercolour Society; USGA = United States Golf Association; USPGA = United States Professional Golfers Association.

Foreword

Golfing Art is a wonderful book for me because the superb pictures it contains reflect the history and the tradition of golf.

I've known Phil Pilley, who has compiled, written and edited it, for more than 20 years and have appeared in many TV programmes and films he has produced, and I was interested recently to replay on my video an interview I gave in one of them. In it I tried to convey the sense of history and tradition I felt – and still feel – as a professional golfer:

> 'To play where the great players have played, to savour all the historic courses, to follow literally in the footsteps of all the legendary past champions ... it's all somehow magical.'

I felt that when I won the 1969 Open championship at Royal Lytham – particularly so, because there I was winning the oldest championship in golfing history. I felt it when the following year I won the United States Open. I've felt it in recent years in the proud moments of victory by the wonderful European team I've had the privilege of captaining.

And I feel it now as I look at the dust-jacket of *Golfing Art* and see the age-old Swilcan Bridge at St Andrews. How many great golfers must have walked over that little bridge, as I have, with all eyes on them and the stone clubhouse of the R & A, the Holy of Holies at the Home of Golf, at the end of the trail!

I cannot claim to be an expert on art, so I'm pleased Mr Pilley has not been too technical or 'arty' in his approach. Instead, he draws our attention to the wealth of paintings and drawings devoted to the game, shows them to us, puts them into context and tells us some interesting stories about them.

By coincidence, I have recently been asked if I would sit for a portrait myself; all very flattering! Perhaps Phil will include the result in some other book in the future! Meantime this book will occupy a special place in my home and ultimately, I suspect, tempt me to plaster my walls with golfing art so that I am surrounded by the tradition of a game I love so much.

TONY JACKLIN

Introduction

This book presents some 60 golfing images, some classic favourites, some seen or published for the first time. Technical dissertation is out, because my aim is to attract more golfers and golf-lovers to the deep reservoir of art that is part of the spirit and tradition of their game and to encourage them to enjoy it as such. The learning for all of us automatically follows.

The sunflowers and irises of van Gogh sell for multi-millions. The sand-blown grass of the golf links portrayed by less celebrated artists comes somewhat cheaper: at top level we are talking in thousands of pounds, not millions. This may or may not put into perspective where golf truly stands in the world of art; it has no relevance to the pleasure experienced by those who appreciate or collect the game's pictures.

Let us consider the monetary value of golf works, then rid ourselves of it quickly for money is not our subject. A painting hanging on a clubhouse wall depicting one of those Dutch games allegedly the precursors of golf has been valued at more than £250,000 – and that says nothing of similar works in the world's great galleries and museums. Rumours suggest an offer of £1 million, reputedly refused, for one privately owned Scottish painting. As this book goes to press a rare Victorian oil due to be shown at a major exhibition at Burlington Galleries in London is being talked about as having six-figure potential.

Generally, though, valuations of works in major British golf collections tend to reach around £30,000, with £3,000 perhaps par for the course and numerous lesser works assessed in the hundreds. Anomalies and surprises persist: a painting described to me this year as a 'silly little oil' was valued that same month at £10,000; a recent sale of memorabilia where estimates were spectacularly surpassed inspired a newspaper writer to wonder whether golfers were going mad!

From this random selection of facts and figures the following conclusions can be drawn. First, as always, beauty and therefore value are in the eye of the beholder; second, outstanding originals now rarely come to market; third, when they do they will attract higher prices than ever before. A boom in golf collecting joined voraciously by the Americans and Japanese as well as Europeans threatens to become a fever and to infect the areas of paintings and drawings as well as those of clubs, balls, literature, sculpture and ceramics, parallel obsessions not covered in these pages. To most people 'sporting prints' means huntin', shootin' and fishin', but this year an expert rated golf prints ahead of all other sports in terms of profit potential. Now, not another word about money!

Selection in this book has been based largely on balance, with an eye toward history, but basically, selfishly, on personal prejudice. Numerical restriction has meant omitting some artists whose work ideally I would have included and some comparatively famous works. Lemuel Francis Abbott's familiar 'Henry Callender' is absent: I felt the formal red-jacket portraits of the eighteenth and nineteenth centuries were already well represented. No Sir Henry Raeburns? I thought there was insufficient golfing content in his skilled portraits of club officers. Whenever possible I have arranged special photography of original paintings or engravings; occasionally I have resorted to reproductions, particularly where originals were untraceable or unavailable. Occasionally a work has sneaked in on historical importance rather than artistic merit.

History? These pictures convey, incidentally, much of the story of golf and some of its social backcloth. Equally they can be misleading. While the Dutch landscape masters were showing their golfing scenes on land and ice in the seventeenth century what was happening in Britain and particularly in Scotland? If you judge from art, nothing. We know differently. The explanation is that in Britain landscape painting did not develop until the next century.

However, the other significant periods are covered: in the eighteenth century the occasional landscape showing golf as a natural, accepted part of the Scottish scene; then the large portraits of distinguished captains commissioned by the well-to-do, sometimes by themselves and presented to their clubs, sometimes commissioned by a club as a tribute to a member; the first, spasmodic prints; the age of the distinguished amateur, with artists portraying influential men who not only played but spread the game towards its Victorian upsurge; gradually, perhaps grudgingly, portraits of the professionals; in modern times an apparent penchant for painting course landscapes with or without action. Why have so few artists attempted and succeeded at showing golfers in action: ie the swing rather than the address? Is there not a paucity of outstanding portraits of the great champions of this century? There are rich compensations.

The high echelons of art may perhaps scorn some works the golf enthusiast will admire. Recently, when an anthology of sporting literature was published, one reaction seemed to be that it was all very well but did it really matter? The golf afficionado who can ally his enthusiasm for play with an enjoyment of the game's art would surely resent such an attitude to his sport and to what he beholds as beautiful about it.

PHIL PILLEY
Shepperton, 1988

Golfers on the Ice near Haarlem

Oil painting by Adriaen van de Velde (1636–72)

12 in × 14⅓ in (30.5 cm × 36.5 cm)

This is one of the many fine seventeenth-century landscapes that include club-and-ball games and add to the conclusion that the Dutch as well as the Scots significantly helped to establish golf. The Dutch games possibly developed from the Roman *paganica*, reputedly played with a club and a ball stuffed with feathers. Versions certainly existed by 1296 and were played in streets, the country and widely, as in this painting, on ice.

Van de Velde was among the early European masters of landscape. He may also possibly have painted 'Ice on the Scheldt', another scene showing players, which hangs in the Royal and Ancient clubhouse at St Andrews. (Van Ostade, van der Neer and particularly Adam van Breen are other possible artists suggested by experts.)

'Golfers on the Ice near Haarlem', dated 1668, hangs in the National Gallery, London. It shows two kilted figures, one of them about to play, and, presumably, their Dutch opponents. This suggests that the game of *colf* in various forms and under sundry names had become a national pastime and that golfing history was strongly influenced by trade between Scotland and Holland – not least perhaps by ships' crews relaxing on Scotland's east coast while waiting to sail with their wool cargoes.

Controversy lingers. 'Gouff' is recorded in Scotland from 1457 as a pastime so popular as to be discouraged by Parliament. The game probably developed in both countries until the eighteenth century. The theory that Scots and Dutch traders adopted each other's games, clubs, balls and phraseology, playing on surfaces ranging from Dutch ice to Scottish coast, is impressive.

Van de Velde's painting, sometimes known as his 'Frost Scene', was engraved, but printed in reverse, by the Frenchman Aliamet under the title *Les Amusemens de l'Hiver* (c1740) and also for a small series of Dutch scenes published by Carrington Bowles in London during the same period.

The Kolven Player

Etching by Rembrandt van Rijn
(1606–69)

3¾ in × 5¾ in (9.5 cm × 14.5 cm)

Rembrandt's etching, impressions of which can be seen in the British Museum and sundry other collections, is frequently known as 'The Golfer' and shows the interior of an inn with a player outside, but scholars name it according to the game they believe it represents. The safest, albeit unsatisfactory label would be *het kolven*, a generic term covering sundry early Dutch club-and-ball games.

Rembrandt's man was probably playing a version akin both to the old court game of 'pall mall' and to *kolf*, which was to become more fashionable in the eighteenth century and was contested in courts, gardens, grounds or alleys attached to inns or country houses. Historically, then, this genre scene may be less relevant to golf history than are the great Dutch landscapes, but Rembrandt's is the most illustrious name on any work related to the game. In this etching his broken yet flowing lines look as though he were using not a needle on wax but a pen.

'The Kolven Player' is signed and dated 1654, when Rembrandt was seriously in debt. Two years later creditors sold his house and put his collection up for auction.

Child Playing Golf

Oil painting by Bartholomeus van der Helst (1613–70)

44 in × 33 in (112 cm × 84 cm)

This painting was formerly attributed to Albert Cuyp, but now to Bartholomeus van der Helst, an outstanding Dutch portrait painter. The inventory of The Edward James Foundation at Chichester, Sussex, where it hangs, describes a 'portrait of a boy playing by the shore'; other sources wrongly have suggested the child is a girl. Who *was* the child? Perhaps the offspring of one of the many wealthy Amsterdam notables who flocked to be portrayed by van der Helst? The painting, frequently reproduced, is by no means the only one of the period which portrays children playing golf-type games.

The details of club and ball in the 'seaside links' location provide more evidence of *colf* (as opposed to the more sedate *kolf*), which by now in its cross-country form had so much in common with our game. Even in phraseology there were similarities: balls could be hit off something phonetically akin to a 'toytee' and in certain versions of the game be holed into a *put* (suggestive of our putt- or pot-hole) instead of to a peg or natural target. And the shout *'Stuit mij!'* ('Stops me') sounded rather like and meant what, until the rules were changed, we called a 'stymie'.

Then, mysteriously, inexplicably, *colf* went out of fashion and existence early in the eighteenth century.

St Andrews

Oil painting by unknown artist

13½ in × 39 in (34.25 cm × 99 cm)

As *colf* in Holland died golf in Scotland grew. The east coast was its hotbed, St Andrews became its spiritual home and this oil on canvas just possibly is the earliest picture of golf being played in Britain.

Controversy surrounds the date, however. At first, research suggested 1760–70, but when the painting, old and needing repair, was donated to the Royal and Ancient Golf Club of St Andrews (R & A) in 1847, the captain's remarks emphasizing its antiquity were, in the view of more recent members, an inference that its origin was earlier. Subsequent opinion favoured between 1680 and 1720; recently an expert, judging the dress, pronounced the work as perhaps 1760 'if all other things were equal'; the R & A's own inventory grudgingly concedes 'circa 1720', but some members still feel the painting may be seventeenth century and one independent valuation and one book have labelled it as such.

The building on the right of the painting is a windmill with its sails removed: something done in the 1760s and also earlier, around 1690.

Golfers beneath Edinburgh Castle

Water-colour by Paul Sandby, RA (1725–1809)

11½ in × 18½ in (29 cm × 47 cm)

This faded water-colour in the British Museum is thought to date from 1746–7, when Sandby was working in Scotland. Until the St Andrews work (previous page) emerged it was generally accepted as by many years the earliest picture of golf in Britain. It may well still be that. Certainly it is a rarity: an eighteenth-century British landscape embracing golf.

Sandby was a draughtsman: topography fascinated him, the Dutch landscape masters influenced him, Gainsborough called him the only man of genius who had painted 'real views from Nature' in Britain. He is credited as the first English artist to practise and popularize aquatint engraving, using resin in liquid form to brush on the copper plate like a water-colour wash.

In this work showing the old Bruntsfield golfing course, where the game had been played at least since the fifteenth century and whose importance declined with the development of Edinburgh, the players seem to be soldiers and have caddies. The artist's collector's mark is at lower right.

Eighteenth-century golf at Bruntsfield beneath the castle is depicted also in an engraving of 1798 by J. Walker after F. Nicholson.

Landscape with Golfers

Oil painting by unknown artist

19½ in × 23 in (49.5 cm × 58.5 cm)

Eyebrows were raised when this work was brought to the notice of British experts in 1988: nobody knew anything about it. The painting hangs in the United States Golf Association's museum at Far Hills, New Jersey, where the curator, Janet Seagle, has been unable to discover anything additional to the inventory description giving the name of John B. Ryerson, now dead, as the donor in 1972 and bearing a 'circa–eighteenth-century' attribution alongside the title, 'Landscape with Golfers'. Ryerson apparently found it in a Florida gallery. Only occasional eighteenth-century golf landscapes have been discovered and suspicion exists about this one both here and indeed at the United States Golf Association (USGA).

Comparison with nineteenth-century non-golf landscapes makes it almost certain, in the editor's view, that the scene represented is Blackheath, England's first golfing centre, dating traditionally from 1608 and on a heath so named because it was a burial place for London victims of the fourteenth-century Black Plague. Golf dealers and collectors feel the work generally and the golfers' poses particularly have the feel of an imaginative, retrospective portrayal, probably painted in the nineteenth century. However, a researcher at the British Museum has agreed with the eighteenth-century theory.

William St Clair of Roslin

Oil painting by Sir George Chalmers (c1720–91)

88 in × 61 in (224 cm × 155 cm)

The first rules of golf as we know them came in 1744 from the Honourable Company of Golfers of Edinburgh, regarded by many as Scotland's earliest* and (until the R & A gradually assumed control) most influential club. Its image has long been one of exclusivity. Even George Pottinger's book 'Muirfield' says that this portrait of a mighty figure in the club's history 'epitomises the elegant, mildly disdainful approach associated with the Company of Golfers'.

Chalmers, who was a member, had studied portraiture with Allan Ramsey and in Rome and was to exhibit at the Royal Academy from 1775 until his death. He shows William St Clair as he was in 1771, one of his four years as captain on the Company's early links at Leith, aged 70. He was also three times captain of the R & A.

St Clair wears the traditional red jacket. His method of playing the old feather ball may look bizarre, but Sir Walter Scott wrote of him from boyhood memories as an heroic, athletic figure: 'The last Roslin (for he was uniformly known by his patrimonial designation and would probably have deemed it an insult in any who might have termed him Mr. Sinclair) was a man considerably above 6 feet, thin-flanked and broad-shouldered, built it would seem for the business of war or chase … In all the manly sports which require strength and dexterity he was unrivalled, but his particular delight was in archery.'

This oil, often reproduced since it and many others were printed in Bernard Darwin's 'A Golfer's Gallery' in 1920, was formerly owned by the Company. They sold it during a financial crisis in the 1830s but possess a fine copy. The original hangs in the Hall of the Royal Company of Archers in Edinburgh.

*The Honourable Company is generally regarded as the oldest organized club with rules, as distinct from possibly earlier, less organised societies such as the Royal Burgess Society of Edinburgh with whom it shared links.

William Inglis on Leith Links

Oil painting by David Allan (1744–96)

51 in × 41 in (129.5 cm × 104 cm)

Inglis, a surgeon, is another of the red-jacketed greats from the Honourable Company of Edinburgh Golfers' past remembered through notable oil paintings. He was captain from 1782 until 1784. In the background on Leith Links may be seen the procession of the silver club, of which Allan did a separate pen-and-water-colour.

The silver club was presented to the Edinburgh Golfers in 1744 by the City of Edinburgh and their first rules (largely the basis of the modern game) were framed for the annual competition for it. Originally, at Leith, the winner became 'Captain of the Golf' and had to present for attachment to the trophy a gold or silver coin or ball. This tradition is maintained, albeit through the elected captains, and there are now four such silver clubs at the Company's present home, Muirfield. In days gone by the announcement of each year's competition was made public by a procession with drums through the city.

Allan, who became known as 'the Scottish Hogarth' through engravings of Roman carnival scenes exhibited at the Royal Academy, completed 'Inglis' in 1787 after his return from Italy, when he painted in houses of the nobility. It hangs in the Scottish National Portrait Gallery and since the Second World War has been engraved by Britain's Lawrence Josset.

William Innes ('The Blackheath Golfer')

Coloured mezzotint after oil painting by Lemuel Francis Abbott, RA (1760–1803)

23½ in × 17 in (60 cm × 43 cm)

This is probably the first English painting of a golfer. Royal Blackheath (as it is now) was England's earliest organized club, documented from 1766 and preceded, as the Honourable Company of Edinburgh Golfers and others had been, by a looser 'society of goffers', dating traditionally in their case from 1608, after James I and his Court brought the game to London from Scotland. The membership continued to be predominantly Scottish.

Abbott was tutor to the sporting artist Ben Marshall and was known particularly for his portrait of Nelson. His oil of William Innes symbolizes a rich man's game. Innes (1719–95), son of a Scot and a prosperous London merchant, wears the uniform of club captain; the caddie, with bottle at the ready, is a pensioner of the Royal Naval Hospital, Greenwich.

The print published by the artist in 1790, uncoloured from a mezzotint engraving by Valentine Green, was the first British golf print. When the impressions began to wear it was printed in colour as here, and finished by hand. Today an uncoloured version can be seen at the British Museum and many collectors own prints and reproductions of various types, hues and qualities. Innes's clothing varies in colour in different versions.

The original was thought to have perished in an eighteenth-century club fire, but in recent times some commendable detective work has added spice to the story. Innes's memorial tablet in London emphasizes his respectability and reports that he and his wife 'had no issue'. King besmirches that legend with allegations of bribery and slave profits, says Innes had nine children by one Agnes Palmer, that the painting (possibly re-captioned as a 'cover up') passed to his family and that a grandson, General Henry Palmer, stated in memoirs that 'the oil painting, full-size, of a gentleman standing in a field holding a club, inscribed "John Innes, Father of the Scottish Golf Club"', was destroyed in Lucknow on 30 May 1857 by the Indian Mutineers.

John Taylor

Oil painting by Sir John Watson Gordon, RA, PRSA (1788–1864)

96 in × 60 in (244 cm × 152.5 cm)

Surely one of the most powerful golfing portraits of all time? Taylor captained the Honourable Company of Edinburgh Golfers for a total of eight years in four terms between 1807 and 1828. He played the first match for wager at Musselburgh, where they eventually moved, the old links at Leith no longer being suitable. The original painting hangs in the clubhouse at Muirfield.

Sir John Watson Gordon was Scotland's leading portrait painter, succeeding his friend and teacher Sir Henry Raeburn, exhibiting 123 works at the Royal Academy and many more at the Royal Scottish Academy. 'John Taylor' recalls the artist's style as praised in *Scottish Painting* by Sir John Caw: 'Whatever it lacks in brilliance it is simple, sincere and at its best gravely beautiful.'

Legend says the caddie, kneeling to tee up the ball on sand as was the custom, was painted by Raeburn, but Raeburn died in 1823 and the portrait was finished in 1830 or shortly before. Another theory is that Sir Henry began the painting and Sir John completed it; yet another is that Raeburn had promised the club he would paint it but died before he could do so.

The formal early portraits are redolent of the freemasonic influence within societies. The red jackets were also ceremonial dining wear and golf at first was more a preface to feasting and conviviality. Had not William St Clair himself in the previous century been Grand Master of the Grand Lodge of Scotland and, like others after him and not only in Edinburgh, been chosen in preference to the 'captain of the golf' to lay the foundation stone of the clubhouse with masonic honours? Freemasonry was all-important.

The first engraving was in 1914 by Will Henderson and W. A. Cox's set of mezzotints published by Gainsborough Galleries in 1926 included, as had Henderson's, 'John Taylor' as well as Abbott's 'William Innes' and 'Henry Callender of Blackheath'. Again there have been many reproductions, but Henderson's and Cox's remain the sole genuinely engraved versions of 'Taylor'.

First Meeting of The North Berwick Golf Club

After oil painting by Sir Francis Grant, PRA (1803–78)

24 in × 37 in (61 cm × 94 cm)

For almost the first time we see action dominate the landscape instead of being incidental to it. This attractive scene, formal yet convivial, was exhibited at the Royal Scottish Academy in 1833, just before Grant made his belated debut at the Royal Academy, a decade before he became the most fashionable portrait painter in Britain and more than 30 years before being made the RA's president.

North Berwick is one of our oldest golfing areas, but the present club was officially founded in 1832. The members shown are Robert Oliphant of Condie (putting), Captain Brown, Colonel Norval, J. Campbell of Saddel, Sir David Baird, a Mr MacDonald of Clanranald, Lord Elcho, G. Wauchope, Mr Carnegie and Mr Stewart of Alderson.

Several of these men appear in Grant's hunting scenes, for which he became well known, and Oliphant, Baird and Campbell were to feature in another fine golf painting a few years hence: Charles Lees's 'The Golfers' (page 36).

Sir Francis Grant, younger son of the Laird of Kilgraston, Perthshire, and married to a niece of the Duke of Rutland, socialised easily with well-to-do sitters such as these. He was interested in golf, was made a member of Blackheath when he went south and 40 years after his North Berwick scene would contribute another notable work to the game: his portrait of John Whyte-Melville (page 42).

The original North Berwick painting was in exhibitions at the Royal Academy in 1939 and the Scottish National Portrait Gallery in 1962, but exhaustive enquiries of eminent art authorities and golf collectors in Britain and the United States had at press-time failed to discover its present whereabouts.

Old Alick

Oil painting by R. S. E. Gallon
(*fl*.1830–68)

25½ in × 19¾ in (65 cm × 50 cm)

'Old Alick' was Alick Brotherston (1756–1840) and the original portrait is owned, as are so many impressive works, by Royal Blackheath. A Scot, he grew to boyhood in another golfing stronghold, Leith, and from there went to sea at 13, serving on a number of Nelson's ships of the line. Subsequently he returned to dry land and became a caddie. Accurate cutting of holes with a knife, as was the early norm, may have been difficult in the stone and gravel of Blackheath: perhaps that is why Alick was promoted to hole-cutter, an unusual sole trade. This was around 1822, several years before hole-cutting equipment was introduced.

Alick, though a labourer, was a revered character at Blackheath: hence, perhaps, the white top hat such as the players wore and indeed the picture itself, by Robert Samuel Ennis Gallon, a London genre and portrait painter and lithographer who exhibited at the Royal Academy between 1830 and 1868. It was presented to the club by Captain Thomas Crosse, its 1856 captain and for many years secretary. On the back of the painting Alick proudly listed the ships and captains in which and under whom he had served. That was probably in 1839. A year later he was dead.

Golfers apparently had begun a fashion in pictorial tributes to their employees at this time. At Blackheath a water-colour by C.E. Cundell of their club-maker Corporal Archibald Sharpe, also top-hatted, already existed, while in Scotland 'Caddie Willie' (next page) was being portrayed.

Blackheath, in fact, has *two* 'Old Alicks' on its walls, the other being slightly smaller.

Caddie Willie

Oil painting by C. H. Robertson
(*fl.* 1835–40)

25½ in × 20 in (65 cm × 51 cm)

'Caddie Willie' was William Gunn (or 'Daft Willie Gunn' as he was unfortunately sometimes referred to), a caddie and character with the Royal Burgess Society of Edinburgh for which claims of 1735 origin have been made and which certainly existed as a club from 1760.

In this odd painting with its strong sense of caricature, completed about 1839, Willie is shown on the so-called links at Bruntsfield. A subsequent lithograph, published by the artist and printed by Robertson and Ballantine of Edinburgh, was dedicated to the 'clubs of Edinburgh and Leith'. The Society members subsequently moved to Musselburgh, where the Company of Edinburgh Golfers also played, but they are now based at Barnton.

Willie appears in garb not unlike that described as his norm: three or four sleeveless jackets with a member's cast-off red coat outside them; underneath, an old fur vest over three or four thinner ones plus three pairs of trousers; on his head, three bonnets sewn together! In 1813 the Burgess gave him 12 shillings after his bed-clothes and other belongings were stolen from the garret where he lived.

The Society bought the painting, which had hung in the 'Golf Tavern', Bruntsfield, for £3 in 1845, but it is recorded that it 'went astray' after being sent on loan for a Glasgow exhibition in 1911. Royal Blackheath now claims the original, it having been presented (as was the case with 'Old Alick') by Captain Crosse, reputedly following his purchase of the work in a Scottish sale!

However, the Royal Burgess now has what appears to be a contemporary version, so it seems likely that Robertson did two paintings. When it was cleaned, re-painting was discovered over earlier work wherein Willie's legs had been longer. Both versions and the lithograph all vary, the castle for example being in a different position in each case. Shown here is the painting as it hangs at Blackheath.

The Golfers

A Grand Match Played Over St Andrews Links

Engraving after oil painting by Charles Lees, RSA (1800–80)

21 in × 33½ in (53.5 cm × 85 cm)

Lees's painting, engraved by Charles E. Wagstaff, renders landscape almost totally subservient to golf, mixes portraiture with activity and gives us the equivalent of today's wide-angle action photograph. This was golf nearly 20 years before the first professional championship. Lees depicts it as a game for the gentry, with caddies, club- and ball-makers the 'professionals'.

Lees, an East-of-Scotland artist, has captured a moment in a match at the R & A's 1841 annual meeting. The ball to the right has been played by Sir David Baird (in black top hat leaning in, left of central group): a fine iron shot from the long grass and heather visible above the crowd on the left. His partner is Sir Ralph Anstruther. Now Major Playfair (next to Baird) has just putted and his partner, John Campbell, smoking, looks on imperiously as the ball runs straight for the hole.

A key (page 126) identifies every person, each painted from a special sitting: hence unusually faithful likenesses. Lees's individual studies can still be seen. Eventually, in 1847, Lees's painting, 'fresh from the easel', went on show at the Edinburgh galleries of Alexander Hill, who had bought it for £400. This original, measuring 4ft 3in × 7ft (129cm × 213cm), is now privately owned by a descendant of one of the spectators.

Wagstaff's black-and-white line engraving was published by Hill in 1850 and can be seen in the Scottish National Portrait Gallery and the R & A collection. Some prints were then coloured and many varied reproductions have appeared, one pleasing one having been published in 1973.

A smaller lithograph published toward the end of the nineteenth century shows sundry differences: some figures, including the horse-riders, are absent and others are in changed poses.

A Golf Match

and

Summer Evening at Musselburgh

Oil paintings by Charles Lees, RSA (1800–80)

A Golf Match: 10 in × 15¼ in (25.5 cm × 39 cm)
Summer Evening at Musselburgh:
10 in × 16⅓ in (25.5 cm × 41.5 cm)

Lees ranks high among golfing artists. Born in Cupar (Fife), he became a pupil of Sir Henry Raeburn and apart from portraits and landscapes did many paintings of sporting life in Scotland.

His oil sketch of the putting scene (top right), now in the R & A collection, was done en route to his ambitious St Andrews work (previous page) and some of the figures were incorporated in the final painting, which is zealously guarded against the eyes of most outsiders by its Scottish owner. Lees's painstaking individual sketches such as this caused the delay between the 1841 subject and the 1847 painting, although the scrapbook of Allan Robertson, one of the caddies in 'The Golfers', offers some evidence that the work was ready in 1844, three years before its normally accepted date.

In 1859 Lees completed his scene at Musselburgh which has qualities reminiscent of the telling light effects he achieved in a fine skating picture 'Sliding on Linlithgow Loch', 12 months previously. Notice how his St Andrews work influenced that of Musselburgh.

Musselburgh was one of the early courses for Edinburgh golfers and when play became impossible at Bruntsfield and Leith many of them transferred there. Today what remains for play is surrounded by a racecourse. At the time of Lees's painting the links were shared by the Bruntsfield and Royal Burgess Societies with the Company of Edinburgh Golfers, whose present-day clubhouse at Muirfield houses this copy. The original is believed to be in North America. Prints are rare: apparently an engraving was being printed in Germany but went missing during wartime.

Allan Robertson

Oil painting by unknown artist (Scottish School, mid-19th century)

30 in × 25 in (76 cm × 63.5 cm)

Robertson (1815–59), a St Andrews man (the caddie to the left in Lees's *The Golfers*), was the greatest player of his time, the first outstanding professional. He was also a renowned ball-maker, following a trade carried on by his family since early in the eighteenth century.

The sombre but impressive oil hangs as part of the R & A collection. The ball Robertson holds would surely have been one of his beloved 'featheries', stamped ALLAN. The clubs? Perhaps 'The Frying Pan', 'The Doctor' or 'Sir Robert Peel' ... because Robertson had such names for those he used!

The first reference to the painting dates from 1894. Sir Alexander Kinloch, whose R & A membership had begun six years before Robertson's death in 1859, drew the club's attention to the 'very good likeness' he had seen in a shop-window and which he felt they might be able to buy for 'well under £40'.

John Whyte-Melville

Oil painting by Sir Francis Grant, PRA (1803–78)

96 in × 54 in (244 cm × 137 cm)

Major John Whyte-Melville of Bennochy and Strathkin-ness, near St Andrews, was a member of the R & A for 67 years. He joined in 1816 when he was 19, was captain in 1823 and was nominated for the captaincy again 60 years later but died before he could take office. Meantime his son George, a Victorian novelist, had been captain in 1851.

Sir Francis Grant painted John Whyte-Melville, in a composition reminiscent of Sir John Watson Gordon's 'John Taylor' (page 28) but embracing a St Andrews backcloth, in 1874, when he was president of the Royal Academy. His flattering style and friendship with the subject produced a portrait of charm, dignity and auth-ority, the caddie reverent in his placing of the ball for the eminent member, but, to judge from photographs, it is short on likeness. Whyte-Melville apparently had broader features: a man presented as a formidable figure in old age by Thomas Hodge's sketch in the Badminton Library golf volume over the caption, 'Two rounds in a gale of wind at 83!'

The portrait, which cost 500 guineas in 1874, a huge sum then, is in the R & A's collection. It was printed as a limited edition oleograph (a reproduction simulating an oil on canvas) during the 1970s.

Allan Robertson and Tom Morris

Water-colour in sepia by Thomas Hodge (1827–1907)

5½ in × 4 in (14 cm × 10 cm)

Hodge, fine player, R & A member and talented amateur artist, has left us a valuable legacy of water-colours and drawings, but his true place in the story of golfing art comes later in this book (p.48). This 1889 sketch from the Badminton golf volume, later to be coloured and copied by others, is not truly representative of his most significant work, because while he observed and drew contemporaries from life 'Robertson and Morris' is demonstrably from an early photograph, Robertson having died 30 years previously. Its inclusion here is due more to chronology and to mark an important milestone in golf history.

Robertson and Morris formed golf's most formidable partnership – and when Robertson faded, Morris, six years younger, was destined to succeed him at the top of the pile. He would live into his late eighties to become revered as 'Old Tom Morris'. He would win four Open championships, establish himself as a skilful club-maker, become keeper-of-the-green at Prestwick and St Andrews and serve the R & A in an honorary capacity until he died.

It is said that Morris and Robertson, to whom the former was apprenticed as a ball-maker, were never beaten in a challenge-match series, but Allan allegedly avoided Tom at singles play after one defeat and they fell out away from the links. The reason? Tom used the new gutta-percha ball, whose advent dealt a blow to Allan's business. In 1851 Morris left St Andrews for Prestwick on the west coast, where he stayed some 13 years before returning.

ALLAN ROBERTSON AND TOM MORRIS

William Park, Senior

Oil painting by John A. T. Bonnar
(exh. 1885–89)

107 in × 70 in (272 cm × 178 cm)

The year after Allan Robertson died the Open championship was born and Willie Park from Musselburgh was the first winner. There were only eight players in 1860, all professionals and all Scots, though one of them represented Blackheath, and the championship comprised three rounds of the 12-hole links at Prestwick, Ayrshire. Later the event was declared 'open to the world', but for years that virtually meant Scotland.

Park's winning score was 174 and Tom Morris, who was to win the next two years and four times in all, was second. Park himself would win three times more, in 1863, 1866 and 1875. In seven of the first eight championships either Park or Morris finished first.

Park, a renowed club- and ball-maker, whose son Willie Junior (twice) and brother Mungo would also win the Open, was in his mid-twenties when he took his first championship, perhaps 30 years before this telling portrait of him against a Musselburgh backdrop. It was first reproduced on the cover of the 1971 Open championship programme and is a treasured part of the R & A collection.

The artist Bonnar, who exhibited 12 works at the Royal Scottish Academy, probably painted Park after he himself moved to Musselburgh from Edinburgh in 1887.

Old Daw

Water-colour in sepia by
Thomas Hodge (1827–1907)

6½ in × 9 in (16.5 cm × 22.75 cm)

A different example of Hodge's work: an atmospheric study of 'Old Daw' Anderson, a character at St Andrews for more than half a century as caddie, ball-maker and greenkeeper.

In the 1850s 'Old Daw' carried for Allan Robertson and Tom Morris, and later for amateurs like George Glennie, captain both of Royal Blackheath and the R & A. It is said he was the first to suggest placing two holes on the same green, thus bestowing on the Old Course one of its unique features. He remained a familiar figure well into the 1890s with his refreshment trolley on the links, where Hodge depicts him at the back of the tenth tee. He died in 1901, aged 80, by which time his elder son, Jamie, had long since won three successive Opens.

Hodge, who originally came from Cornwall, thrice won the R & A Autumn Medal competition and once the Spring Medal. He did many illustrations in the Badminton Library's golf volume and, though geographically parochial, concentrating on St Andrews and often relying on photographs, his artistic range was considerable: from his gold-tinged painting of the St Andrews October Meeting (1862) to water-colour portraits such as that of Glennie (1880) and delicate, perceptive little sketches of numerous other St Andrews personalities, many identifiable by idiosyncrasies of style observed by the artist.

Hodge would sketch on scraps of paper or backs of envelopes; he exhibited only once at the Royal Scottish Academy (1880); but he and the man we are about to meet were the first prolific specialist golfing artists at a crucial time of the game's history: the great Victorian boom of inland and seaside golf motivated by, among other factors, the railway, the cheaper and improved 'gutty' ball and the invention of the lawn-mower.

Young Tom's Last Match

Water-colour by Francis Powell Hopkins (1830–1913)

8 in × 12¾ in (20.5 cm × 32.5 cm)

Hopkins (or 'Major S' as he signed many water-colours, including this one), ranks with or above Thomas Hodge as a golfer-artist recording the personalities and play of the late nineteenth century when golf began its surge to wider popularity. Here, according to his annotation on the painting, he has captured a moment of history and pathos: the last match played by Young Tom Morris, son of Old Tom and possibly the game's greatest talent.

It is the winter of 1875 at St Andrews. Behind Young Tom are his four Open victories (1868, 69, 70 and 72) and his outright win of the original championship belt. But also behind him, only a few weeks past, is the death of his wife in giving birth to their still-born child.

Captain Molesworth, RN, an outstanding character of the time and an inveterate gambler, has backed his son Arthur for £100 to beat Tom over six rounds, the young champion to concede six shots a round. Old Tom looks on as his boy fetches up some of his prodigious skills, pitching and stopping the ball dead on the ice-hard turf cleared of snow and comfortably winning the match.

Less than a month later, on Christmas Day, Young Tom will be dead, aged 24. The sculpture over his grave is reminiscent of him as painted by Hopkins. Perhaps this freezing day on the links contributed to the broken heart and consequent lack of self-care generally accepted as the causes of death. That, at least, is the legend behind the picture.

Match at Blackheath, 1869

Wood-block engraving after Frederick Gilbert (*fl.* 1863–91)

9½ in × 13½ in (24 cm × 34 cm)

Down south, by 1869 the Blackheath Club had a new clubhouse, a top Scottish professional, an extended course (seven holes instead of five, three rounds in competition), year-round activity and a changed philosophy: golf was more important than dinner and claret. This was a microcosm of golf's development. Whereas once Blackheath had been England's only club, now there were about 30 and in 20 years the total would be nearly 400.

Publications like the *Graphic, Illustrated London News, Illustrated Sporting and Dramatic News* and others were now taking an interest both in word and picture. This portrayal by a local Blackheath illustrator reflects the new enthusiasm and inevitably, via its black and white, the more down-to-earth, all-weather aspects of golf on the Heath: a windy, flinty, hazardous test over gravel pits and roads and on rough, small greens still not much different from cut fairways.

The Heath obviously had become an increasingly dangerous place for the public to cross. The course was thus becoming outmoded both by size and social circumstance. Eventually the club would move. But not yet.

Golf at Blackheath, 1875

Oil painting by Francis Powell Hopkins (1830–1913)

21¼ in × 44½ in (54 cm × 113 cm)

Hopkins, unlike his contemporary Hodge, observed golf far and wide. At Blackheath he painted this scene on the first tee with Greenwich Park in the background, indicating the blaze of colour that would light the course in a scene such as Gilbert's (previous page).

The membership represented much influence. About to drive is the 1874 captain, James L. Bennet, and having his ball teed up is Colonel Hegan Kennard, MP, who succeeded him in 1875, was a member for 60 years and was prominent in the founding or infancy of other clubs, becoming captain, also, at Hoylake, Wimbledon and Sandwich, and president at Westward Ho! He was largely responsible for Blackheath and other clubs becoming 'Royal' in title.

A key exists naming everyone in the painting (page 126), but the most interesting figures are those of Robert Kirk, the Scottish professional and club-maker from St Andrews (sixth from left), whose salary was £78 per annum, and George Glennie (thirteenth from left), who joined Blackheath in 1853, became a significant administrator there and, partnered by a Captain Stewart, won for them the 1857 Grand Foursomes Tournament at St Andrews, which was contested by 10 other clubs, all Scottish (as indeed were Glennie and Stewart and so many Blackheath members). Glennie is also portrayed at Blackheath painted by Heywood Hardy, RA, and John Ballentyne, RSA.

The Tee Shot

Oil painting by Francis Powell Hopkins (1830–1913)

23¼ in × 41½ in (59 cm × 105.5 cm)

One of the most pleasing oils of the period, signed and dated 1877 and having strong relationships with 'Golf at Blackheath' (previous page) of two years earlier. The artist is the same and the location, Westward Ho!, is the links of the Royal North Devon club, one of many that Blackheath members helped found or supported. The Blackheath influence is clear: seven of the figures appear also in 'Golf at Blackheath', including the ubiquitous Glennie (behind boy caddie, centre right), and Kennard (seated behind next caddie).

Hopkins's sketches as 'Major S' had created a demand for something more ambitious and the Blackheath and Westward Ho! oils were his immediate answers. 'The Tee Shot' was commissioned by John Dun (driving), captain of Royal Liverpool at Hoylake, another 'Blackheath-assisted' club, whose son presented the painting to Royal North Devon. In 1988, potentially the most valuable golf picture to come on the market for several years, it was seen as a centre-piece of the big exhibition, 'Golf – a Royal and Ancient Game', at Burlington Galleries, London.

Standing in the foreground ready to drive next is Captain Molesworth, a founder-member, and fourth from left is Major Hopkins himself, making a characteristic 'Hitchcock appearance'.

Hopkins had left the Army in 1864, come to live and fish in Devon and taken up golf (about which he wrote for *The Field* as 'Shortspoon'), without becoming particularly good at it; yet he painted 80 or more works, mostly water-colours, whose personal subjects are accurately portrayed and which give him claims, in the opinion of his supporters, as the first artist frequently to show golfers actually playing rather than in static positions.

Like Hodge, Hopkins does not seem to have had formal training, nor apparently did he exhibit; but he had a talent for composition and figures and a true feeling for golf and golfers.

Ladies' Match at Westward Ho!

Oil painting by Francis Powell Hopkins (1830–1913)

8½ in × 18 in (21.5 cm × 46 cm)

Mary Queen of Scots played golf, it is said (the late Henry Longhurst, doyen of the game's essayists, described her to the editor ominously as the *first* lady golfer to be beheaded!), and various artists have portrayed the tradition. As examples, a drawing by Amedée Forestier published in *The Illustrated London News* in 1905 imagines her at St Andrews in 1563 and Reginald Heade, who exhibited at the Royal Academy in the 1930s, did an oil painting placing her at the Truro club.

The first women's clubs date from the 1860s and that at Westward Ho! has claims to be the first, having been formed in 1868. This is one year after the St Andrews ladies, but the claim is that the latter used only a putting green. At Westward Ho! they also used putters only but played on their own nine-hole course, the holes varying between 50 and 150 yards. As Hopkins suggests, the women were encouraged and helped by the men, who no doubt also erected the silk tent for their use. It was a decorous pastime: ankle-revealing was taboo and on windy days the ladies wore elastic bands around their dresses at knee-level to prevent their skirts blowing about.

Again Hopkins has left us a sensitively composed and painted oil, signed and dated 1880. With many Hopkins works, it featured in the 1988 Burlington Galleries exhibition.

A Hazard on the Ladies' Course

Woodblock engraving after drawing by Lucien Davis, RI (1860–1941)

11¼ in × 17 in (28.5 cm × 43 cm)

Davis drew this in 1890 for *The Illustrated London News*, for whom he was a principal artist for 20 years. The original was in black and white and there have been many coloured prints and reproductions of R. Taylor's wood-block engraving, ranging from this attractive version to a recent gaudy greetings card bearing Davis's name on its front and 'artist unknown' on its back!

Women's golf was spreading, it was no longer 'putters only', and Davis drew his scene on Minchinhampton Common, Gloucestershire, the year a nine-hole ladies' course was established there. It is an accurate representation of the seventh tee on that original course, which is no longer in play but still recognizable with its adjacent folds and old stone workings between the five-way road crossing known as 'Tom Long's Post' and the 'Halfway House' inn. There are plans to re-create the scene in 1989, when Minchinhampton Golf Club celebrates its centenary.

Davis, Liverpool-born and art master at St Ignatius College, London, was a portrait, landscape and figure painter and illustrator who exhibited 37 works at the Royal Academy and depicted many sporting scenes. His illustrations appeared in the Badminton Library volumes on cricket, lawn tennis and billiards and he drew scenes of women playing games, notably hockey and cricket, other than golf.

Historically, this work (sometimes known as 'Golfing on Minchinhampton Common') is interesting in that the caddie carries a bag, a new invention. Aesthetically it is a pleasing scene, though the drawing of the swing is suspect. The defences are that this was golf before 1900 and that Davis may have been trying to suggest the remarkable action of Lady Margaret Scott, who lived nearby, won the British Ladies' championship in its first three years (1893–5) and was so supple that at the top of the backswing her clubhead, instead of being in line with the target, was pointing directly down at the ball, her right elbow 'flying'.

Golf at St Andrews

Etching after W. G. Stevenson, RSA (1849–1919)

14½ in × 24½ in (37 cm × 62 cm)

Prints of this detailed work etched by Clive Murray were published by the Fine Art Society in 1892 and show some of the most influential characters and finest players of the time on the Old Course.

Among those watching Willie Fernie, the 1883 Open champion, in action on the left are Horace Hutchinson (fourth from left), twice Amateur champion, who had recently edited the Badminton golf volume, and the Rt Hon. Arthur J. Balfour, MP (fifth from left), future Prime Minister, whose example helped golf become fashionable.

From left to right in the next group watching Willie Park, Junior, the 1887 and 1889 Open winner, putting are Dr J. H. Blackwell, from a notable St Andrews golfing family; Hugh Kirkaldy, Open champion the year before the print was published; J. E. Laidlay, Amateur champion that same year; Andrew Kirkaldy, outstanding character and runner-up to brother Hugh in the Open, a championship in which he was destined to finish second four times; John Ball, Junior, first amateur and first Englishman to win the Open; Old Tom Morris; and Willie Park, Senior.

On the right are the Rev J. McPherson and Bob Ferguson, who had won three successive Opens in the previous decade. Tee-boxes (from where the caddie is getting sand for teeing-up) appear for the first time, apart from that shown in the sketch of 'Old Daw' (page 49).

Nostalgia of a more recent vintage wafts through the air – in the smoke from a distant train near a St Andrews station knocked down in the 1960s and replaced by a British Transport hotel!

63

Dr Laidlaw Purves Playing at Wimbledon

Oil painting by William E. Pimm
(*fl.* 1890–1910)

16 in × 24 in (40.5 cm × 61 cm)

This hitherto virtually unknown painting turned up recently, causing considerable interest and detective work. Where was the setting? Wimbledon Common? Ashdown Forest perhaps? And who were the players?

At press-time it was intended to catalogue the painting under the above title for the 1988 Burlington Galleries exhibition, it having been deduced that the man putting was Dr W. Laidlaw Purves, MD, a Scottish stalwart of the Royal Wimbledon club, wearing his traditional red jacket. The other player is believed to be Arthur Molesworth, whom we have already seen at St Andrews.

The present Royal Wimbledon club until 1907 golfed only on the common, where the wearing of red as a warning and safeguard for the public was obligatory from 1892 and has remained so for players there. The club members continued to use and share the common until 1915, even though they had by then moved to their own course nearby. Molesworth, however, is not wearing red, the precise site of this sixth hole had not yet been identified on the common as we went to press (although an old plan suggests the sixth as the only hole likely to have had these surrounding features) and apparently sheep did not graze on the common during the period suggested for the painting: between 1890 and 1900.

Pimm, a London painter who for a time lived in Putney just down the road from Wimbledon, exhibited at the Royal Academy between 1890 and 1910. He was basically a figure and animal painter and also did portraits and miniatures.

The theory that the player in action is Purves can be tested against the portraits of him by John Collier at Wimbledon and (next page) Sandwich, Kent.

Dr W. Laidlaw Purves

Oil painting by The Hon. John Collier (1850–1934)

71¼ in × 47½ in (181 cm × 121 cm)

Purves (1843–1918) was a member of three big pioneer clubs, R & A Royal Blackheath and the Hon. Company of Edinburgh Golfers, but more prominently of Royal Wimbledon and Royal St George's, Sandwich, where this 1896 portrait by Collier, a prominent London artist who exhibited 130 times at the Royal Academy, can now be seen. Purves was another of the influential men and yet another Scot behind the spread of the game in England towards the end of the last century.

Professionally he was a doctor, specializing in eye diseases; privately he was irascibly obsessive about golf and won many important club trophies, the last of them in 1914 when he was 71 and had a handicap of 3. His Wimbledon membership began sourly when he was in a major row about marking his partner's card and ended sadly after sundry rebuffs and a committee decision to let a professional second-guess his designs for the new 1907 course. But in between he was elected captain in 1897–8, spent much time evolving rules and handicapping systems, encouraged women players and, with Issette Pearson and other members of the Wimbledon Ladies' club, was a force behind the 1893 meeting that led to the Ladies' Golf Union being formed. His other great contribution was in founding new clubs – as we are about to see.

Members of Royal St George's, 1892

Oil painting by Allen C. Sealy (*fl.* 1873–93) and Charles Spencelayh HRBSA, RMS, BWS (1865–1958)

29½ in × 59½ in (75 cm × 151 cm)

The Royal St George's club at Sandwich, Kent, was founded in 1887, its pioneer being Laidlaw Purves (see previous page). This typical 'links-land' where the sea had long since receded and with its mass of sand-blown grass and huge dunes became what Purves envisaged when he discovered it a year or two previously: a seaside links for affluent Londoners, comparable with the testing coastal terrain of his native Scotland and several cuts above any inland course. In 1894 it would become the first English course to house the Open championship and two years earlier, when this painting was done, staged the Amateur.

More than 60 members and two wives are in the line-up: now an anonymous collection but including some of the most successful professional men in the country at that time. Purves, the first captain, stands immediately above the kneeling caddie, next to (also in brown) W. R. Anderson, who with Henry Lamb (absent), a fellow Scot and Wimbledon member, helped him get the project off the ground. The putter is A. D. Blyth, a future captain; the tall man standing above the lady on the right is the Hon. Ivo Bligh, England's cricket captain 10 years previously when he brought back from Australia the urn containing the Ashes now kept at Lord's; and behind him and his neighbour is Ramsay Hunter, a Scottish greenkeeper who assisted in the making of the course. The editor, when a BBC producer in the 1960s, met the boy caddie, bringing him back to the course in his nineties for a TV programme. (For key see p.126).

Of the artists who combined on this work, commissioned and presented to the club by a member, Allen Culpeper Sealy was a London landscape and genre painter and Charles Spencelayh, who came from Kent, specialized in figures, portraits and miniatures, being noted for his eye for detail. Both exhibited at the Royal Academy.

The First Club on the Continent

Oil painting by Allen C. Sealy
(*fl.*1873–93)

19¾ in × 30 in (50 cm × 76 cm)

Sealy, having with Spencelayh painted the Royal St George's members, crossed the Channel to portray those of Pau, in the Basses-Pyrenees, southern France. This charming scene signed and dated 1893 resulted.

Pau is the oldest club on the continent of Europe, dating from 1856. The first people to play there had been Scottish officers of Wellington's army towards the end of the Napoleonic Wars (1815). Men such as they returned as tourists years later and the club stems directly from the establishment of a fashionable British colony. The founders were the Duke of Hamilton, Colonel Hutchinson, Major Pontifex, Colonel Anstruther and Archdeacon Sapte, who saw it as a haven where they and their like could spend the winters.

The presence of the women is a reminder that they had had their own nine-hole course at Pau since the early 1880s. However, the painting is not historically accurate as mixed play was not then allowed there.

The well-to-do members must have been enthusiastic to be portrayed in their French setting because Hopkins as well as Sealy was commissioned to paint there. The key to this work was lost during the German occupation of the club.

Medal Day at St Andrews, 1894

Oil painting by unknown artist

60 in × 108 in (152 cm × 274 cm)

This huge oil painting, sometimes known by other titles, shows Arthur James Balfour, the future Prime Minister, playing himself in as captain of the R & A at the 1894 Autumn Meeting: a nerve-wracking moment in which, scrutinized by the membership, the captain drives off the first tee. Balfour, despite all, hit a fine drive.

Balfour's celebrity status made him a much-portrayed figure on the golf course: hence this detailed work, bought (apparently with some reluctance at first) by the R & A from Dickinsons, the print publishers, who had arranged the painting and issued a print in 1898, at the beginning of the century. Unlike Charles Lees, the artist did not have personal sittings but painted his figures from photographs of nearly 200 members and others.

A complete key exists (page 127) identifying 191 prominent personalities, including many of those we have seen in paintings at Blackheath, Westward Ho! and here at St Andrews, making it clear how concentrated the circle of influence in the game still was. Old Tom Morris tees the ball; A. F. Macfie, the first Amateur champion, is in the foreground, extreme left; J. H. Taylor, the Open champion, is in the group on the steps on the right; Freddie Tait, the great amateur who that day won the Medal, stands hand on hip in the foreground towards the left; Andrew Greig, the starter, peers from his box.

The First Amateur Golf Championship held in America, 1894

Coloured lithograph after drawing by Everett Henry (1893–1961)

16 in × 11 in (40.5 cm × 28 cm)

First championship or not, this lithograph dates only from 1931, made by E. Currier for a series in *Fortune* magazine. Nor, according to record books, was this 1894 event the first US Amateur Championship. Nonetheless this somewhat rudimentary work qualifies on grounds of historical interest and anecdote.

Pipe in hand on the left is John Reid, to whose memory as 'father of golf in America' the work is dedicated. Reid, who had emigrated to the New York suburb of Yonkers from Scotland, had in boyhood seen the dawn of the golfing boom, and in 1887 his friend Robert Lockhart brought back for him from Tom Morris's shop in St Andrews some clubs and gutta-percha balls. The result a year later was the St Andrew's Golf Club, America's first organized club, though not the first place where golf had been played.

The club was founded by Reid and his friends, who played successively on a cow pasture originally of three holes, a six-hole lay-out in an apple orchard and nine holes on farmland. Before they moved again the event recalled by Henry was staged.

Elsewhere better, longer courses had been laid out: not least in Chicago, where golf meant the dictatorial, controversial Charles Blair Macdonald, obsessed by the Scottish game since college days at St Andrews and destined to contribute hugely to the game's advancement. In 1894 the Newport club staged an 'open' stroke-play event involving 20 players. Macdonald played, lost by a stroke to W. G. Lawrence and swore stroke-play was no way to decide a championship.

In October that year Reid's club hosted a match-play tournament to find the true amateur champion. Macdonald lost to Laurence Stoddart at the first extra hole of the final, then refused to accept either Stoddart or Lawrence as champion because they had merely won clubs' invitational events. The outcome was the setting-up of official championships under the USGA, in whose museum this lithograph showing Macdonald striking and Stoddart watching now hangs.

John Ball, Junior
Oil painting by R. E. Morrison
(1852–1925)
51½ in × 37¼ in (131 cm × 94.5 cm)

Robert Edward Morrison, a portrait and genre painter born on the Isle of Man, moved to Liverpool and his life there was contemporaneous with the triumphant deeds of the local amateur John Ball, Junior, of whom, in 1899, he painted this sombre portrait. The Royal Liverpool club, Hoylake, commissioned the work to mark Ball's fifth Amateur championship, secured that year at Prestwick.

Ball's father, a good golfer himself, ran the Royal Hotel, the original clubhouse at Hoylake where young Ball learned and played. In 1890 the son won the Open, the first amateur and first Englishman to do so; he went on to win the Amateur championship eight times. And he did it with style: 'I have derived greater aesthetic and emotional pleasure from watching Mr. Ball than from any other spectacle in any game', wrote the golf journalist Bernard Darwin.

Morrison exhibited 41 times at the Royal Academy from 1884 and his portrait of Ball fittingly hangs in the Hoylake clubhouse.

Match at Duddingston, 1898

Water-colour by J. Michael Brown (*fl.*1880–1916)

9½ in × 15 in (24 cm × 38 cm)

By the 1890s golf had become so popular among the 'right' people that advertisers and publicists were latching on to it, setting a pattern that remains (see pages 124 and 125). The Life Association of Scotland, some of whose executives were keen players themselves, decided to issue calendars featuring golf scenes and did so for 25 years from 1892.

The artist who became synonymous with the series was J. Michael Brown, an Edinburgh painter of landscape and river scenes whose Royal Academy exhibits included in 1890 a golf work, 'On Leven Links, Fifeshire'. His work, with its nostalgic photographic atmosphere and striking likenesses, though frequently formal in its parading of personalities, serves as a valuable record of championships, matches, players and fashions. The scenes were printed in sepia.

Brown's Duddingston scene for the 1899 calendar recalls a match played at the Edinburgh course on 25 March the previous year between two Amateur champions, Freddie Tait (putting) and Leslie M. Balfour-Melville (club under arm, right), and two professionals, Willie Auchterlonie, the 1893 Open winner, and little Ben Sayers from North Berwick. This would appear to have been something of a 'jolly' for the bankers and insurance men of Scotland: all the spectators identified, many probably members of the Insurance and Banking Golf Club, came from those professions.

Ladies' Championship at Aberdovey, 1901

Water-colour by J. Michael Brown (*fl.* 1880–1916)

9½ in × 15 in (24 cm × 38 cm)

Another Life Association of Scotland calendar, featuring the only time the British Ladies held their championship at Aberdovey in Wales. The winner was Molly Graham (putting), from Hoylake, who beat Rhona Adair (fifth from left excluding caddie), the defending champion from Royal Portrush, Northern Ireland, 3 and 1. First from left of those seated is May Hezlet, also from Royal Portrush, who won the title three times (1899, 1902, 1907) and in centre-background is John Jones, the Aberdovey greenkeeper.

Three places further on, next but one to T. H. Miller, whom she later married, is Issette Pearson, honorary secretary of the Ladies' Golf Union (LGU), twice runner-up in the championship and a prime mover in the forming of the LGU. (For key see page 126.)

Mixed Foursome

Photolithograph after water-colour by A. I. Keller (1866–1924)

15¾ in × 11¾ in (40 cm × 30 cm)

Keller, a noted illustrator and member of the American Water-Color Society, was commissioned to paint this pleasant scene for the cover of the March 1900 *Ladies Home Journal*. The original hangs in the PGA World Golf Hall of Fame in Pinehurst, North Carolina, a lithograph having been published in 1973, and measures 24 in × 18 in (61 cm × 46 cm).

Golf had spread fast in the United States, among women as well as men. Keller was displaying the game as a winter pastime, with red balls used on a snowy course, but at a more serious level the ladies had had their national championship under the aegis of the USGA since 1895, the same year as the men. Mrs Charles Brown won that first title in 69 + 63 = 132 ... but the course was nine holes!

Frederick Guthrie Tait

Oil painting by J. H. Lorimer, RSA, RSW, RWS (1856–1936)

120 in × 60 in (305 cm × 152.5 cm)

Lorimer painted this portrait from photographic evidence after Lieutenant Freddie Tait was killed in 1900 whilst leading his company of the Black Watch in the second Boer War. The result is striking in overall effect when one sees it hanging in the R & A's collection, although controversial in certain aspects: golfers have asked why Tait should reach out for a club when he had another under his arm, while the R & A, who commissioned the work, called back Lorimer several times to improve the likeness.

Lorimer was an Edinburgh artist who exhibited 43 works at the RA and 123 at the RSA. The portrait of Tait, a little too idealistic in some people's views, was, however, painted in the style of a tribute to one of the finest and most popular amateur golfers in history, who had died in action: a hero.

Tait was Amateur champion in 1896 and 1898, while in the Open he twice finished third and was three times leading amateur. He was an outstanding match-player and a formidable driver: it is said he once hit a gutta-percha ball to carry 280 yards and also drove one 341 yards on a frozen fourteenth hole on the Old Course.

After Freddie died they found in one of his pockets a letter marked with a paw print of his beloved terrier Nails, portrayed waiting behind his master who gazes steadfastly into the distance in Lorimer's painting.

Old Tom Morris

Oil painting by
Sir George Reid, PRSA, HRSW
(1841–1913)

46 in × 34 in (117 cm × 86.5 cm)

Old Tom had been portrayed in countless scenes, but in 1899, as Tom neared 80, the editor of *Golf Illustrated* asked: 'Why has no good portrait been painted? It will be nothing short of a national disgrace if the Grand Old Golfer's features are not handed down to posterity in a worthy manner. Sir George Reid, President of the Royal Scottish Academy, would, I feel sure, make a grand picture of the veteran, for he has such a head as Sir George excels at painting.'

Accordingly Sir George, Scotland's leading portrait painter, whose sitters included most of the distinguished Scots of his time and who exhibited 17 works at the Royal Academy and 125 at the Royal Scottish Academy, was brought in. He asked Tom to take up position with his club but Tom merely held it in his right hand. 'What sort of position is that?' the artist wondered. 'Ah,' said Tom, 'I'm just waiting for the other man to begin.' And it is said that when he was shown the finished work he gazed on it silently, then said, 'Well, the cap's like mine.'

For all that, the portrait in the R & A collection is a splendid study of Old Tom at 81. It has the silvery, atmospheric feel yet vivid characterization and powerful expression for which Reid was renowned. A gravure was published in 1903 and Tom signed a limited edition of 50.

This was by no means the last portrayal of Morris. For example, there is a 1905 pencil drawing of him bare-headed by J. Lessells, a pen-and-ink by A. R. Ramsbottam circa 1910, two years after his death, and more modern attempts, notably by Britain's Arthur Weaver.

Harold Hilton

Oil painting by Richard Jack,
RA, RI, RP (1866–1952)

49½ in × 39½ in (126 cm × 100.5 cm)

Harold Hilton (1869–1942) was the natural successor to John Ball, Junior. He, too, learned and played at Hoylake. He, too, won the Open as an amateur, the second to achieve the feat and one of only three ever to do so. That was in 1892, the first year the championship was contested over 72 holes. Hilton, however, surpassed Ball in winning the Open again in 1897. He was Amateur champion four times between 1900 and 1913, having thrice been runner-up in the 1890s, and in 1911 held the British and US titles simultaneously.

Again, like Ball, Hilton is well represented in golfing art. This 1913 portrait by Jack, a widely travelled, Sunderland-born artist with 25 exhibits at the Royal Academy, hangs in the Royal Liverpool clubhouse. Its formality and portrayal of Hilton bare-headed contrasts strongly with a 1903 'Spy' cartoon showing him cigarette in mouth, short-peaked cap on back of head (page 123), to say nothing of Hodge's little pen-and-wash at the R & A or J. J. Inglis's painting, also at Hoylake, of Hilton's 5ft 7in figure, to quote Bernard Darwin, 'flinging himself at the ball with almost frantic abandon'.

The Triumvirate

Oil painting by Clement Flower
(*fl.* 1899–1913)

60 in × 40 in (152.5 cm × 101.5 cm)

Commissions for portraits of contemporary players had been confined almost exclusively to the depicting of amateurs. But by now three great professional champions had risen in Britain and in 1913 as Jack was painting the amateur Hilton they, too, were being portrayed.

J. H. Taylor (left), James Braid (centre) and Harry Vardon became known as 'The Great Triumvirate' because they dominated golf from the mid-1890s to the First World War. Between them they won the Open championship 16 times in 21 years and Vardon's record of six Opens still stands.

Flower, who exhibited at the RA, was scratch at Westward Ho! and played at various other clubs, was commissioned by *Golf Illustrated*. It was decided that Vardon's drive ('the acme of grace and beautiful body-balance', said the magazine) should be shown on the second tee of the Old Course at St Andrews. Flower painted the setting on the spot, then took his 6 ft canvas to Le Touquet, where Vardon, on holiday, posed twice daily for a week. For the finishing touches Vardon went to Flower's Bushey, Herts, studio, where Braid and Taylor also sat.

Flower felt that Taylor should be shown on the tee with his renowned mashie, but a critic complained that this would imply he had given up the first hole. 'Oh, I don't know,' said Taylor, 'Why shouldn't I have holed my pitch?' And a writer commented, 'As he actually did so in a gale during the last round of this year's Open at Hoylake, the idea may well be allowed to pass unchallenged.'

After five months the painting was complete and publicized as 'the first really great golfing picture of modern times'. Flower directed an engraving, 250 artist's proofs (26 in × 19 in) signed by him and the players being issued at the start of 1914. In the last two decades three limited editions have been published, the first two from 1914 proofs and the last, in 1983, reproduced from the original onto canvas. The original is part of the R & A collection.

JOHN HENRY TAYLOR
Open Champion
1894.1895.1900.1909.1913.7/10 1896.

JAMES BRAID
Open Champion
1901.1906.1905.1908.1910.

HARRY VARDON
Open Champion

CLEMENT
FLOWER
1913

A Caddie to the Royal and Ancient

Engraving after W. Dendy Sadler, RBA (1854–1923)

16 in × 11½ in (40.5 cm × 29.5 cm)

An apparently jarring anachronism amid the jackets, caps and plus-fours of the era we have reached, just before the First World War. Nonetheless, this engraving by James Dobie of a work sometimes known by other titles such as 'A Winter Evening' dates from 1914. Prints have been struck at various times since, notably in 1926 and 1972, some with a remarque and facsimile signatures of artist and engraver.

Dendy Sadler, a genre painter from Dorking, Surrey, who exhibited 51 works at the Royal Academy from 1873, had a penchant for painting costume pieces from the eighteenth or early nineteenth century period: sentimental in approach but often excellent in execution. He was also known as an equestrian artist and produced only about five golfing scenes. His work is represented in the Tate and also in Manchester and other provincial galleries.

Lloyd George at Walton Heath

Water-colour by J. Michael Brown
(*fl.* 1880–1916)

9½ in × 15 in (24 cm × 38 cm)

By 1913 even Brown's Life Association of Scotland calendar works were being printed in colour and the 25-year series ended in this patriotic flourish in 1916, the middle of the First World War.

The scene shows David Lloyd George, the Liberal politician, playing the seventeenth hole at Walton Heath, Surrey, where he was a member, in 1915. Next year he will become Prime Minister and remain so until after the war is won; meantime he seeks relaxation from his responsibilities as Minister of Munitions and Secretary of State for War.

Looking on are James Braid, who won the last of his five Open championships in 1910 and was Walton Heath's professional for 45 years until his death in 1950; Herbert W. Fowler, the golf architect who created the course; and Lord Riddell, who owned it.

Life Association of Scotland

Michael Brown

95

The Prince of Wales
Oil painting by Sir William Orpen, RA, RWS, RHA, RI (1878–1931)

80 in × 40 in (203 cm × 101.5 cm)

The R & A commissioned this painting to mark the club captaincy of the Prince, later Edward VIII and after his abdication Duke of Windsor, in 1922. It was completed and hung only after problems. Acrimonious exchanges between club and artist occurred because of delay in delivery: the portrait was not completed until June 1927, nearly five years after the Prince had driven himself into office. Also, the members pressed for the Prince to be portrayed wearing the captain's formal red tailcoat but eventually had to settle for the Shetland pullover presented to him on a visit to Lerwick.

For all that, however, Orpen, a fine Irish-born, London-based artist who portrayed many distinguished subjects, had been an official First World War artist and been knighted in 1918, has left a work that holds an honoured place in the R & A collection. The Prince was and would remain a keen golfer here and elsewhere – an honorary member of the club from 1913 and its patron in 1936 – and Sir William's portrayal, although not to everyone's approval, captures the boyish features that made him an idol of millions, something of the character that gave him appeal yet perhaps contributed to the abdication and a hint of melancholy mingled with the innocence.

Nancy, Lady Astor at North Berwick

Oil painting by Sir John Lavery, RA, RSA, RHA (1856–1941)

24½ in × 29½ in (62.25 cm × 75 cm)

North Berwick, one of the traditional haunts of golf on Scotland's east coast, is a recurring scene in the sport's art. It is a backdrop as important, or almost, as the personalities shown playing in front of it in works from Sir Francis Grant's 'First Meeting of the North Berwick Club' (1833), through John Smart's 'Dyke Hole' and the Life Association's calendar 'North Berwick', both published in 1893, to twentieth-century efforts like Heywood Hardy's mixed foursome scene (1903), Michael Brown's 'Perfection Bunker' (1910) and this privately owned oil painting by Sir John Lavery signed and dated 1924.

To golfers North Berwick is one of the old 'homes', and its professionals such as Ben Sayers and holes like the short 'Redan' have been featured by artists and photographers alike. To many people it became a fashionable place to be seen: to be photographed on the first tee at North Berwick was a thing to be done, and how much better to have been painted!

Significantly, Sir Francis Grant and Sir John Lavery, who exhibited 154 works at the Royal Academy and 97 at the Royal Scottish Academy, were leading society painters in their respective eras, each with all the talents to justify that status and the flattering style and temptation towards dissipation of those talents that, so to speak, went with the job. Lavery, on one of his visits to North Berwick, which he painted more than once, completed this scene, probably for his host, showing Nancy, Lady Astor. The first woman MP to take her seat in Parliament, she was an enthusiastic golfer, frequently played at North Berwick and became president of the LGU.

Walter Hagen

Oil painting by Frank C. Bensing
(1893–1983)

39 in × 29¾ in (99 cm × 75.5 cm)

Walter Hagen was America's, indeed the world's outstanding professional of the 1920s. Bensing was a Chicago-born magazine illustrator and increasingly a portrait painter whose subjects included Herbert Hoover and Joseph P. Kennedy.

Hagen (1892–1969) was a genuine 'character' as well as a golfer. His sayings and deeds have become clichés and legends: 'Never hurry, never worry, always take time off to smell the flowers' ... 'I never wanted to be a millionaire, just to live like one' ... At Deal, Kent, they would not let him, a professional, change his shoes in the clubhouse, so he did so in his Rolls Royce parked outside. He won the US Open twice (1914 and 1919), the Open in Britain four times (1922, 24, 28 and 29) the USPGA championship five times (1921, 24, 25, 26 and 27), and captained the American Ryder Cup team several times well into the 'thirties.

Bensing's portrait from the 1950s, based on photos, may be uncharacteristic in that Hagen is so formally dressed, whereas in his prime he had been known for the snazzy pullovers, cardigans, plus-fours and black-and-white shoes that helped kill off the old golf-jacket syndrome. But it captures the man, with a hint of the sterner character that helped him raise the status of the professional in a snobbish society.

The painting hangs in the museum of the USGA, to whom it was presented in 1958 by Robert A. Stranahan.

Bobby Jones

Oil painting by J. A. A. Berrie, RCA
(1887–1962)

42 in × 52¼ in (107 cm × 133 cm)

Robert Tyre Jones, Junior (1902–72), the American amateur, has been the subject of several portraits in his own country and Britain. He is the game's folk-hero, revered years after his death not only for his playing record but for his dignity, sportsmanship, sense of life's priorities and bravery when illness ultimately confined him to a wheelchair.

He won four US Opens (1923, 26, 29 and 30), tying twice but losing in play-offs, and three British Opens (1926, 27 and 30), plus five US Amateur championships and one British. In 1930 came his 'grand slam' of all four titles, the British and American Amateurs and Opens, surely a record for ever. Then, at 28, he retired.

As with Hagen, his words and actions are indelible in the sporting legend. Once, unseen as he tried to hack out of rough, he accidentally moved the ball. Accordingly he penalized himself a stroke and duly lost the championship by that one self-inflicted penalty. He was surprised he was congratulated. 'You might as well praise a man for not robbing a bank,' he said.

This portrait is by John Archibald Alexander Berrie, a club golfer who exhibited five works at the Royal Academy and, though travelling widely, lived in Liverpool, near where the portrait hangs at Hoylake. It was here Jones played in his first British Amateur, aged 19, and won the 1930 Open that helped him to his 'grand slam'. Probably the painting was to mark that historic feat.

The familiar clean features are those of Jones as he was in his prime, when he forsook the strain of competition to concentrate on his profession as a lawyer and to help Clifford Roberts, a New York investment banker, found the Augusta National club in his native Georgia, and begin the Masters tournament.

Henry Cotton
Oil painting by J. A. A. Berrie
(1887–1962)

60 in × 50 in (152 cm × 127 cm)

Sir Henry Cotton, MBE, who died aged 80 in 1987, is renowned in British golf as the player who in the 'thirties broke an American stranglehold on our Open championship which, through Hagen, Jones, Sarazen, Tommy Armour and their like, had lasted a decade. Cotton first won in 1934 at Royal St George's, motivating a string of 12 British and Commonwealth victories interrupted by the Second World War and one victory immediately afterwards by Sam Snead. He also won in 1937 at Carnoustie and 1948, when he was 41, at Muirfield, and is the only British player since the First World War to have taken the title more than once.

Artist John Berrie, though he played much of his golf on Merseyside, was a member at Langley Park, Kent, where Cotton was professional from 1926 (at the age of 19) until January 1933. It appears that the Langley Park membership commissioned Berrie to do this painting and presented it to Cotton in 1938 amid some acrimony, because Berrie had portrayed him against not their club but that of Ashridge, Hertfordshire, where Henry was now the pro! There was even a dispute as to who should pay for the frame: Berrie declined so Langley Park again paid.

The painting may be open to criticism as rather flat and clinical, yet it hangs at the R & A, to whom Cotton gave it, as a faithful record of what he looked like in his prime. The immaculate bearing reminds us that, as with the American Hagen and earlier British players such as J. H. Taylor, Cotton did much in a class-conscious world to raise people's respect for the professional. To the end he continued in golf as architect, author and teacher, and with his eyes on the game's future was largely responsible for the Golf Foundation and its work for juniors.

Berrie portrayed several members of the Royal Family, Sir Winston Churchill, jockeys including Sir Gordon Richards, and – besides Jones and Cotton – golfers Bobby Locke and Dai Rees.

Golf at East Brighton

Oil painting by Conrad Leigh
(born 1883)

15½ in × 20½ in (39.5 cm × 52 cm)

The blessed atmosphere of a game of golf on an empty course amid the horrors of war strikes the senses on seeing this little-known painting and the 'circa 1940' date ascribed for it in the 'Royal and Ancient Game' exhibition in 1988. Seen in that context, the sea adds dramatically to the mood. In the summer of 1940 Britain's troops across the Channel were evacuated from Dunkirk and the Battle of Britain was waged in the air.

Some East Brighton members tend to date the painting immediately *prior* to the war, say 1935–9, because there is no sign of the barbed wire and paraphernalia of an anti-aircraft site placed hereabouts during hostilities. No matter when Leigh painted and signed the scene, he has given to golfing art an unpretentious yet evocative and comparatively rare view of the game at club level on one of the lesser-known courses. The players are putting on what members believe was East Brighton's tenth hole and the village of Ovingdean nestles between them and the St Dunstan's building in the distance.

Leigh was a local Brighton illustrator whose work appeared in *Strand*, *Woman* and other magazines, and who took to painting principally landscapes, figures and sporting subjects.

Ben Hogan

Oil painting by J. Anthony Wills
49½ in × 39½ in (126 cm × 100.5 cm)

If Hagen, Sarazen, Cotton and company were the professional stars of world golf before the Second World War, America's Benjamin William Hogan was the outstanding figure just after it. If Bobby Jones is a legend for his sportsmanship, Hogan became one for his courage when he battled back from a car accident that nearly killed him in 1949 to win the US Open in a play-off the following year.

The artist Wills, from Houston, Texas, painted the hero from life at a course in the Fort Worth area, where Hogan lived, in 1967. The champion was then in his fifties and his posing for the artist represented a departure from his customary reluctance to associate with anything smacking of publicity.

Hogan won four US Opens (1948, 50, 51 and 53), one British Open (1953), two Masters (1951 and 53) and two USPGA championships (1946 and 48). The painting was given to the USGA by Marvin H. Leonard.

Brancaster

Oil painting by Julian Barrow
(1939–   )

20 in × 30 in (51 cm × 76 cm)

Julian Barrow, Cumberland-born, London based and frequently travelling to the Middle East and America, is one of several British artists – Arthur Weaver, James Fletcher Watson, Kenneth Reed and William Binnie are among others – who have included golf-course portrayal among their works in recent years and who have become known through limited edition prints. He paints exclusively in oils and concentrates mainly on landscapes and country houses. The Queen, the Queen Mother and Prince Charles all own works by him.

Barrow does not play golf, but his landscapes are evidence of a sympathetic 'feel' for the subject. He has painted at Sunningdale, Royal St George's, The Berkshire, and Walton Heath and, in 1970, the Royal West Norfolk links at Brancaster: the work, privately owned, shown here, looking back towards the eighteenth green and first tee.

Gleneagles

Oil painting by Arthur Weaver
(1918–   )

23½ in × 35¼ in (59.5 cm × 89.5 cm)

Arthur Weaver, a London-born artist who moved to Wales after the Second World War, has been commissioned by organizations and people as varied as British Railways, United States cattle-breeders, Marylebone Cricket Club and the National Museum of Wales. He has done illustrations, reproductions, landscapes and figures; Texas oil wells, American cotton-fields, a centenary Test Match at Lord's and an African diamond mine. However, he is best known to most people these days as a painter of golfing subjects. His work is represented in the R & A collection, the USGA museum and many clubs here and abroad.

Some paintings issued by modern artists, of whom Arthur Weaver is of course one, may be held by traditionalists and golf observers to be too geometric and clean-cut truly to represent the wildness of golf courses and the hurly-burly of championships with huge crowds and technical paraphernalia, but others have been acclaimed and few would quibble at this oil painting of the Gleneagles Hotel courses, Perthshire, signed and dated 1979.

The scene is the approach to Tinklers Gill, the twelfth hole on the Queen's Course, while in the distance are the bunkers of Tappit Hen, hole 12 on the longer King's Course and the highest point of the layout.

The 18th at Pebble Beach

Oil painting by LeRoy Neiman
(1927–   )

24 in × 42 in (61 cm × 106.5 cm)

Neiman's brand of art disappoints, even repulses, many who admire the dignity, depth, detail and studied formality of the old works, but its colour and sense of immediacy attract others. Some, calling his work superficial, purely illustrative or colourfully grotesque, do not consider him even a representative of golfing art, but to the American sporting public his is the name that immediately comes to mind. All might agree that he is and has been built into golfing art's best 'marketer'.

Neiman, now New York based, is a 'media' figure: appearing on TV, painting Olympic events 'live', contributing for more than three decades to *Playboy* magazine, issuing highly popular prints in limited editions. In the gobbledegook of the world he inhabits impressionist, social realist, action painter, abstract impressionist and pop artist are among the labels applied to him.

His personal subjects are frequently portrayed in wider scenes at dramatic moments. He makes quick sketches, then develops them into oils, applying the paint thickly, often not on canvas but board covered with polymer ground and using commercial enamels that permit fast strokes and, he says, the impression of action. The vivid colours, he contends, emphasize the spirit of the fleeting scene within the atmosphere of these highly spectacular modern American events. It is a jolting contrast to the static encapsulation of action represented by Lees's 'The Golfers' nearly a century-and-a-half earlier.

'The 18th at Pebble Beach' depicts a scene from the 1983 Bing Crosby Pro–Am at that spectacular Californian course. The players are (left to right) former President Gerald Ford, Jack Nicklaus (putting), Tom Watson and Clint Eastwood. Extreme left is Bob Hope in red plus-fours and yellow top, and further to the right in white is Neiman sketching.

12th Green, Augusta National

Oil painting by Arthur Weaver (1918–)

24 in × 36 in (61 cm × 91.5 cm)

Virtually every new golf painting completed by the prolific Weaver is now being sold in the United States, where he is regarded by golfers as their sport's leading specialist artist. Although a series of retrospective 'Golf Personalities', starting with Old Tom Morris, Young Tom Morris and Willie Park, Senior, has recently been published in America, Weaver's reputation is based on landscapes of courses and scenes depicting modern players in action in major championships here and in the United States: small figures in wide-angle views of greens, generally during putting. In the States, because of the distances involved, he relies considerably on photographic evidence along with his sketch-book.

The beautiful, lush, manicured course of Augusta National in Georgia, home of the Masters, has provided a favourite setting for his work, and many of his scenes there have been issued as prints. This painting, completed in October 1985 and sold in Philadelphia, is typical.

The Ailsa Course, Turnberry

Water-colour by Kenneth Reed, FRSA (1941–)

16½ in × 26½ in (42 cm × 67.25 cm)

Turnberry's Ailsa course on the west coast of Scotland became an Open championship course in 1977, when Tom Watson edged out Jack Nicklaus in a memorable finish. With its holes stretching out towards and past the lighthouse and the granite dome of Ailsa Craig off-shore it is the most spectacular of the championship links. Kenneth Reed's painting was completed in 1985 and is now in the United States.

Reed, a keen golfer, was born in Hexham, Northumberland, and began specializing in sporting subjects. In Britain he has painted locations including Sunningdale, Gleneagles, Muirfield and St Andrews, showing the 'Home of Golf' in various conditions from 'stormy' to 'sunset'. In the United States he has portrayed Pebble Beach, Cypress Point, Spyglass Hill, Del Monte, Shinnecock Hills, Augusta National and the Olympic Club, San Francisco. A departure into lawn tennis produced 'No. 5 Court, Wimbledon', during the All-England Championships.

The Seventeenth

Water colour by William Binnie, DA (1941–)

26 in × 19¼ in (66 cm × 49 cm)

This final painting, before we look at some of the cartoonists, caricaturists and advertisement-illustrators who have taken golf as a theme, brings us almost full circle in chronology: a modern look at one of the oldest golfing grounds, St Andrews.

The featured hole is the 461-yard par 4 seventeenth, the 'Road' hole, perhaps the most difficult in championship golf. First the drive: shave the hotel on the right, where the old black railway sheds used to stand, risking out-of-bounds for the best approach to the green; or play safe to the left? Then the treacherous second shot: can you keep out of the bunker and stop on the green? Over the years countless players have met disaster in bunker or on road, and even in recent Open championships one recalls Japan's Nakajima taking 9 after being in the sand and America's Tom Watson losing his chance of a sixth title by hitting a long iron over the green, across the road and up against the wall on its far side.

William Binnie, from Dundee, was awarded the Stewart Prize in the Royal Scottish Academy's painting competition in 1963. He specializes in landscapes and florals and 'The Seventeenth', painted in 1985 with predominant use of body-colour, is among those in print.

Fittingly, here at St Andrews, the 'Home of Golf', the R & A will soon open, adjacent to the clubhouse in the distant left, a museum where the public will be able to see clubs, balls and other historic memorabilia including fine watercolours and original documents.

The Caricaturists
'Spy' and 'Lib'

Among the painters of formal portraits, landscapes and action scenes have lurked the caricaturists, and none more significantly than 'Spy', two of whose efforts are reproduced opposite. 'Spy' was Sir Leslie Ward, RP, RA (1851–1922), grandson of the horse-painter James Ward. He exhibited works in oil, water-colour and black-and-white, but achieved fame by his paintings and cartoons of public figures in *Vanity Fair*, the magazine for which he worked for 40 years until it ceased publication in 1914.

'Spy's' works were also published in supplements and albums, notably those titled 'Men of the Day'. By 1890 the leading amateur personalities of golf were considered worthy of that description and his portrayal of Horace Hutchinson, twice Amateur champion (the original water-colour is in the USGA museum), began an intrusion of eight golfing subjects into the *Vanity Fair* series.

The next golf caricature, in 1892, was done not by 'Spy' but by 'Lib', the Italian Liberio Prosperi. His subject was John Ball, who that year won the third of his eight Amateur championships. The original signed water-colour appeared at the 'Royal & Ancient Game' exhibition in London during 1988.

Thereafter 'Spy' was responsible for six more golfers, his style varying considerably in the degree of outright caricature. In 1903 came both Mure Fergusson and Harold Hilton (under the title 'Hoylake'); in 1906 Robert Maxwell, another Amateur champion; in that and the following year acceptance of professionals as 'men of the day' with the inclusion of J. H. Taylor ('John Henry') and James Braid ('Jimmy'); finally, in 1909, came H. Mallaby-Delley ('The Prince of Princes'). 'Spy' was also to portray the future Prime Minister, Lloyd George, club in hand, for *The World* magazine.

The *Vanity Fair* prints were chromolithographs, then photolithographs and are regularly seen.

John Ball, Junior – *by 'Lib'*

'Hoylake' (Harold Hilton) – *by 'Spy'*

'John Henry' (J. H. Taylor) – *by 'Spy'*

The Cartoonists

When any activity becomes popular the cartoonists and advertisers cash in. These two pages provide a tiny sample of the vast number of cartoons and advertisements that followed in the wake of golf's progress once it began to take off in the latter part of the nineteenth century.

Caricatures go back long before the days of 'Spy' (previous page): John Kay's 'Cock of the Green', depicting Alexander McKellar and dating from 1803 on the old Edinburgh course of Bruntsfield, is the classic case. Humorous captioned cartoons were widely published during the Victorian boom. *Punch* carried one in 1886, for example, and hundreds of artists and illustrators followed: notably 'George Pipeshank', R. M. Alexander (both active towards the end of the century), Harry Furniss (1854–1925), Tom Browne (1872–1910), John Hassall (1868–1948), Frank Reynolds (1876–1953), Lawson Wood (1878–1957), Harry Rountree (1880–1950), Charles Crombie (1885–1967) and H. M. Bateman (1887–1970). The United States threw up parallels: not least A. B. Frost, who, like several of the British artists, included more serious scenes in his golfing repertoire.

These have been followed in turn by countless modern cartoonists throughout the golfing world. Indeed the artists far outnumber their themes: failure, frustration, bad temper, rules, lady golfers and the jangling of nerves under the eyes of lookers-on!

'A bad lie'

— *Lawson Wood* (1930s print)

THE MAN WHO MISSED THE BALL ON THE FIRST TEE AT ST. ANDREWS.

— *H. M. Bateman* (The Tatler, 1925)

'Anyway, it's better to break one's ——— clubs than to lose one's ——— temper!'

— *Harry Rountree* (Punch)

The Advertisers

Golf, during its history, has been used to advertise products from tea to tobacco, biscuits to Bovril, toffee to toothpaste, Ovaltine to Guinness. On the opposite page, two samples. The figure of Johnnie Walker was created in 1908 by Tom Browne, RBA, RI. In 1910, the year of Browne's death, Johnnie appeared playing sports, one of which was golf, and few advertising campaigns will achieve the immortality of this one created more than three-quarters of a century ago.

'Tongue-tied'

— Lawson Wood (1930s print)

The Dream of the Golfer who forgot his GUINNESS a day

"GUINNESS IS GOOD FOR YOU"

H. M. Bateman, who played or watched golf at Reigate Heath, Walton Heath, St Andrews and other venues, provided the cartoon above for a promotional booklet in 1937.

This 1930 advertisement with its excruciating pun was printed in the form of a showcard.

GOLFING 1820.

A reminder of the Johnnie Walker 'Sporting Prints' series by Tom Browne, the errand-boy who became a celebrated artist, illustrator and cartoonist.

Key to illustrations

The Golfers (see page 36)

1. Sir John Muir Mackenzie of Delvin, Bart.
2. Sir John Murray Macgregor, Bart.
3. O. Tyndall Bruce, Esq. of Falkland.
4. Sir Charles Shaw.
5. Colonel Playfair, St. Andrews.
6. The Earl of Eglinton and Wyntoun.
7. Robert Lindsay, Esq. of Straiton.
8. James Hay, Esq., Leith.
9. The Earl of Leven and Melville.
10. Allan Robertson, Golf-Ball Maker, St Andrews.
11. John T. Gordon, Esq., Sheriff of Midlothian.
12. John Sligo, Esq. of Carmylie.
13. Hamilton Anstruther, Esq.
14. John Whyte Melville, Esq. of Mount Melville.
15. Lord Berriedale.
16. F. Blair, Esq. of Balthayock.
17. The Master of Strathallan.
18. John Grant, Esq. of Kilgraston.
19. James Wolfe Murray, Esq. of Cringletie.
20. James Ogilvie Fairlie, Esq. of Coodham.
21. John Hay, Esq. of Morton.
22. Sir David Baird of Newbyth, Bart.
23. Major Playfair of St. Andrews.
24. Thomas Platton, Esq., W.S.
25. Sir Ralph Anstruther of Balcaskie, Bart.
26. John Balfour, Esq. of Balbirnie.
27. The Hon. David Murray.
28. John Stirling, Esq., St. Andrews.
29. James Condie, Esq., Perth.
30. Colonel Murray Belches of Invermay.
31. James H. Dundas, Esq., W.S.
32. James Blackwood, Esq., W.S.
33. Robert Oliphant, Esq., W.S.
34. Charles Robertson, Esq.
35. Sir Norman M. Lockhart of Lee and Carnwath, Bart.
36. Robert Chambers, Esq.
37. Colonel Moncrieff.
38. Lord Viscount Valentia.
39. John Campbell, Esq. of Glensaddel.
40. Henry Macfarlane, Esq., M.D., Perth.
41. Willie Pirie, a well-known Caddie.
42. Sir John Campbell of Airds, Bart.
43. The Hon. Henry Coventry.
44. George Cheape, Esq. of Wellfield.
45. William Dun, Golf-Ball Maker, Musselburgh.
46. Captain David Campbell.
47. William Peddie, Esq., of Black Ruthven.
48. William Wood, Esq., Leith.
49. George Dempster, Esq. of Skibo.
50. William Goddard, Esq., Leith.
51. Robert Patullo, Esq., St. Andrews.
52. Sandie Pirie, a well-known and popular Caddie.
53. Ginger-beer Girl.
54. The City of St. Andrews.

Golf at Blackheath (page 54)

From left: Frederick Gilbert, W. Meikle, Visitor, W. Brand Sr., J. W. Adamson, Bob Kirk (professional), J. A. Rucker, J. H. Morley, The Hon. Charles Carnegie, D. G. Brown, J. Bett, N. J. Reed, G. Glennie, J. Sawyer, W. Kiner, Flowery (caddie), J. L. Bennet, T. Bett, J. W. Hyde, T. Marsh, caddie, W. McCandlish, Col. E. H. Kennard, unknown, Peter Steel, Stephen Smith, Frank Gilbert.

Members of Royal St George's (page 68)

From left: J. Strong, W. Carr, J. B. Joyce, E. Banbury, H. Carter, Dr. Harrison (at back), W. D. Bovill, R. H. Pringle, G. G. Kennedy, W. C. Harrison, H. C. Blyth, R. H. Caird, S. Mure Fergusson, C. Plummer, J. R. D. Hill (at back), W. Rutherford, B. Davis, T. Taylor (at back), C. Thompson, W. Grieve, H.H. Turner, R. Clutton, S.S. Schultz, Colonel Cox.

A. D. Blyth (putting), General Hughes Elliott, R. H. Hedderwick, A. Denman, T. L. Ridpath, C. F. Grundtrig, T. R. Mills, W. Morley, Mrs. A. C. Adams, E. F. Tylecote (white cravat), H. Acklom (furthest back), Hunter, Mrs. H. C. Blyth, The Hon. Ivo Bligh (immediately behind Mrs Blyth), J. Oswald, F. Welman, G. E. B. Kennedy, Cumming MacDona, Colonel Shewell (striped jacket), G. Chatterton, A. A. Cornmon, C. E. Nesham, W. L. Purves (next to bearded man), Caddie, W.R. Anderson.

Group in foreground on right: G. R. Luxford, A. C. Adams (check cap), Colonel Jones, H. C. Rhodes, A. L. Tweedie, The Hon. R. C. Grosvenor (further back). Group at back on right: S. Abernethy, W. O. Pell, Professor N. Lolkyer, Felix Barry, H. Nicholls (bearded), R. G. Nicol, R. Lawson, Capt. Austin, J. C. Wadham.

Ladies championship at Aberdovey (page 80)

Adults, from left: Mrs Wilson Hoare (Westward Ho!), Miss Bryan (Minchinhampton), Mrs Miller (championship committee), Miss E. Neville (Worcs.), Miss Rhona Adair (Royal Portrush), Miss B. Thompson (Scarborough), Miss M. A. Graham (Hoylake, champion), John Jones (greenkeeper), Miss Walker Leigh (Foxrock), Miss S. Whigham (Elysian), Miss I. Pearson (hon. sec. LGU), Talbot Fair, T. H. Miller (vice-presidents LGU), Mrs Phillips (Northampton), Miss M. Hezlet (Royal Portrush), Mrs Ames (Royal Winchester), Miss E. Cobbold (Great Yarmouth), Miss J. Magill (Co. Down), Mrs Hulton (hon. treasurer LGU), Miss Lister (Headingley), A. Pearson (referee), Mrs Stubbs (Barham Downs), Miss M. E. Phillips (Princes).

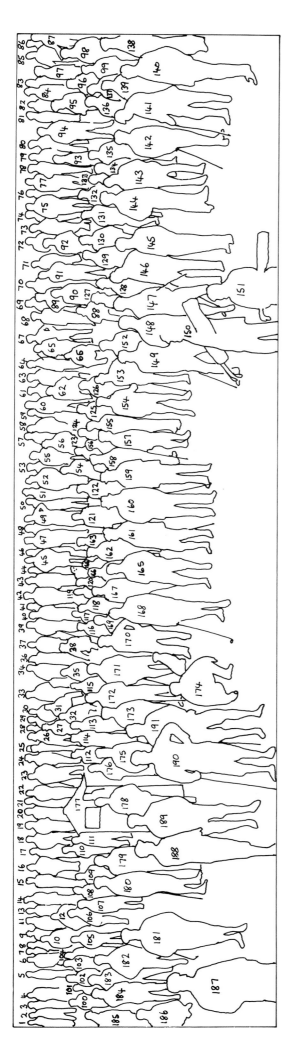

Medal Day at St Andrews – 1894

THE TERRACE

1. Charles Leslie Melville
2. Major W. B. Craigie
3. W. C. Thomson
4. D. Argyll Robertson, M.D.
5. Rev. W. W. Tulloch, D.D.
6. A. N. Stewart
7. W. A. Henderson
8. A. E. Henderson
9. H. B. Simson
10. E. C. P. Boyd
11. Lt.-Col. A. Boyd
12. Hugh M. Alexander
13. James Mellor
14. Col. J. McGregor Kerr
15. W. B. Skene
16. Hon. G. Waldegrave Leslie
17. L. B. Keyser
18. W. D. Bovill
19. John Goff
20. E. S. Balfour Melville
21. Major-General Grahame
22. R. Dalyell, C.B.
23. Major-General G. H. Moncrieff
24. Col. E. H. Kennard
25. J. Lindsay Bennet
26. John Dun
27. *R. Hon. Sir H. E. Maxwell Bart., M.P.*
28. J. Tulloch Tarver
29. F. Tarver
30. Lt.-Col. W. Marshall
31. C. E. S. Chambers
32. *R. N. Fairlie*
33. H. Seton-Karr, M.P.
34. C. L. Anstruther
35. H. A. Bethune
36. John Penn, M.P.
37. Rev. W. W. Tulloch, D.D.
38. A. N. Stewart
39. E. C. P. Boyd
40. Lt.-Col. A. Boyd
41. Hugh M. Alexander
42. James Mellor
43. Col. J. McGregor Kerr
44. Lieut.-Gen. E. M. Playfair, R.A.
45. F. C. Crawford
46. F. D. A. O. Wolfe Murray
47. David I. Lamb
48. D. B. Wauchope
49. T. T. Oliphant
50. Viscount Dalrymple
51. James G. Baird Hay
52. Sir Alexander Kinloch, Bart.
53. R. Whyte
54. Capt. W. Cunningham
55. Ernest Lehmann
56. J. L. Ridpath
57. Professor G. G. Ramsay
58. Hon. A. H. Grosvenor
59. Capt. J. A. Middleton
60. Bruce E. Goff
61. Surgeon-Major Duncan
62. E. L. I. Blyth
63. A. Marshall
64. E. M. Protheroe
65. H. H. Longman
66. A. Gray
67. J. W. B. Pease
68. C. S. Grace
69. Rev. A. K. H. Boyd, D.D., LL.D.
70. Henry Cook
71. — Robb
72. A. R. Paterson
73. R. H. Johnston
74. W. G. Bloxsom
75. A. G. G. Asher
76. A. Cowan
77. C. E. Gilroy
78. Earl of Kinnoull
79. F. Burgoyne Wallace
80. Capt. John Stott
81. W. R. Kermack
82. G. Tertius Glover
83. Stuart Oliphant
84. *W. Park*
85. *W. Auchterlonie*
86. *H. Kirkaldy*
87. *D. Rolland*

ON THE STEPS

88. Stuart Grace
89. Thomson Glover
90. Major Chalmers
91. E. A. Burchardt
92. H. G. Fellowes Gordon
93. *A. Denman*
94. J. L. Low
95. *W. F. E. Blackwell*
96. Wm. Tulloch
97. *J. Taylor*
98. Harry Cheyne
99. F. M. Heriot

ON THE GREEN

100. G. C. Wylie
101. P. C. Dalmahoy
102. Maj.-Gen. P. Dalmahoy
103. J. W. Moir, M.D.
104. Robert Moir, M.D.
105. *Rev. W. Proudfoot*
106. *Rev. J. Kerr*
107. W. L. Purves, M.D.
108. *N. Foster*
109. Sir Uthred Dunbar, Bart.
110. Col. W. Cleland
111. Lt. W. Maitland Dougall, R.N.
112. W. Logan
113. *Capt. H. J. Fairlie*
114. J. O. Wallace
115. R. Hon. Lord Moncrieff
116. *Capt. H. Kinloch*
117. Sir A. B. Hepburn, Bart
118. F. Kinloch
119. J. Wharton Tod
120. E. B. H. Blackwell
121. John Oswald
122. Major C. H. Morris
123. John C. Watson
124. Rev. E. D. Prothero
125. G. M. Cox
126. Rev. R. A. Hull
127. A. N. Ross
128. C. F. Deans Dundas
129. J. H. Aitken
130. Col. R. T. Boothby
131. R. T. Boothby
132. Col A. D. Fordyce
133. John Murray
134. James Cunningham
135. M. P. Fraser
136. W. H. Fowler
137. J. H. Blackwell
138. E. H. Buckland
139. Peter Wood
140. W. Gilbert Mitchell-Innes
141. E. R. H. Blackwell
142. H. S. Colt.
143. Andrew Lang
144. H. S. C. Everard
145. W. M. De Zoete
146. W. E. Fairlie
147. Frank A. Fairlie
148. T. Mackay
149. S. Mure Fergusson
150. *'The Skipper'*
151. *Corstorphine*
152. W. J. Mure, C.B.
153. Sir David Baird, Bart
154. Gilbert Mitchell-Innes
155. C. Hutchings
156. *W. Dunsford*
157. C. Anderson
158. R. B. Sharp
159. Robert Cathcart
160. Alexander Bethune
161. *J. Ogilvy Fairlie*
162. Sir J. L. E. Spearman, Bart
163. D. W. Lambe
164. F. W. Fison, M.P.
165. Leslie Balfour Melville
166. James Balfour Melville
167. Major D. A. Kinloch
168. Rt. Hon. A. J. Balfour, M.P.
169. Sir Ralph Anstruther, Bart.
170. Major Robert Bethune
171. Rt. Hon. Lord Kingsburgh
172. B. Hall Blyth
173. *Rt. Hon A. Graham Murray, Q.C., M.P.*
174. *Tom Morris*
175. Hon. Stormont Finch-Hatton
176. *Aytoun*
177. *Andrew Greig (Scorer)*
178. *P. C. Anderson*
179. Hon. Ivo Bligh
180. C. Eric Hambro
181. Capt. W. H. Burn
182. William Gordon
183. *A. J. Robertson*
184. *J. P. Croal*
185. *A. Kirkaldy*
186. W. T. Linskill
187. A. F. Macfie
188. Horace G. Hutchinson
189. J. E. Laidlay
190. F. G. Tait
191. Alexdr. Stuart

The names in italics are those of non-Members of The Royal and Ancient Golf Club

Index

Abbott, Lemuel Francis 9, 26, 28
Aberdovey 80
Adair, Rhona 80
Advertisements 124
Alexander, R. M. 124
Aliamet, engraver 10
Allan, David 24
Anderson, 'Old Daw' 48
Anderson, W. R. 68
Anstruther, Sir Ralph 36
Ashridge Golf Club, Hertfordshire 104
Astor, Nancy, Viscountess 98
Auchterlonie, Willie 78
Augusta National Golf Course 116

Baird, Sir David 30, 36
Balfour, Hon. Arthur J. 62, 72
Balfour-Melville, Leslie M. 78
Ball, John, junior 62, 76, 122
Ballentyne, John 54
Barrow, Julian 110
Bateman, H. M. 124
Bennet, James L. 54
Bensing, Frank C. 100
Berrie, J. A. A. 102, 104
Binnie, William 120
Blackheath
    see Royal Blackheath Golf Club
Blackwell, Dr. J. H. 62
Bligh, Hon. Ivo 68
Blyth, A. D. 68
Bonnar, John A. T. 46
Braid, James 90, 94, 122
Brancaster, Royal West Norfolk links 110
Breen, Adam van 10
British Museum 12, 18, 20, 26
Brotherston, Alick 32
Brown, J. Michael 78, 80, 94, 98
Browne, Tom 124
Bruntsfield 18, 34, 38, 124

Callender, Henry 9, 28
Campbell, John 30, 36
Caricaturists 122
Cartoonists 124
Chalmers, Sir George 22
Collier, Hon. John 66
Cotton, Henry 104
Cox, W. A., engraver 28
Crombie, Charles 124
Crosse, Captain Thomas 32, 34
Cundell, C. E. 32
Currier, E. 74

Darwin, Bernard 22, 28
Davis, Lucien 60
Dickinsens 72
Dobie, James, engraver 92
Duddington 78
Dun, John 56

East Brighton Golf Club 106
Eastwood, Clint 114
Edward, Prince of Wales 96
Edward James Foundation, Chichester 14

Ferguson, Bob 62
Fergusson, Mure 122
Fernie, Willie 62
Fine Art Society 62
Flower, Clement 90
Ford, Gerald 114
Forestier, Amedee 58
Fowler, Herbert W. 94
Frost, A. B. 124
Furniss, Harry 124

Gallon, R. S. E. 32
Gilbert, Frederick 52
Gleneagles 112
Glennie, George 48, 54, 56
Gordon, Sir John Watson 28
Graham, Molly 80

Grant, Sir Francis 30, 42, 98
Green, Valentine, engraver 26
Greig, Andrew 72
Gunn, William 34

Haarlem 10
Hagen, Walter 100
Hardy, Heywood 54, 98
Hassall, John 124
Heade, Reginald 58
Helst, Bartholomeus van der 14
Henderson, Will, engraver 28
Henry, Everett 74
Hezlet, May 80
Hilton, Harold 88, 122
Hodge, Thomas 42, 44, 48, 88
Hogan, Ben 108
Honourable Company of Edinburgh Golfers (inc.
    Muirfield) 22, 24, 28, 38, 66
Hope, Bob 114
Hopkins, F. P. (Major S) 50, 54, 56, 58
Hoylake, see Royal Liverpool Golf Club
Hunter, Ramsay 68
Hutchinson, Horace 62, 122

Illustrated London News 58, 60
Inglis, J. J. 88
Inglis, William 24
Innes, William 26, 28
Insurance and Banking Golf Club 78

Jack, Richard 88
Jones, Bobby 102
Jones, John 80
Josset, Lawrence, engraver 24

Kay, John 124
Keller, A. I. 82
Kennard, Colonel H. 54, 56
Kirk, Robert 54
Kirkaldy, Andrew 62
Kirkaldy, Hugh 62

Ladies' Golf Union 66, 80
Laidlay, J. E. 62
Langley Park Golf Club, Kent 104
Lavery, Sir John 98
Lees, Charles 36, 38
Leigh, Conrad 106
Leith Links 24, 28
Lessels, J. 86
'Lib' (Liberio Prosperi) 122
Life Association of Scotland 78, 80, 94, 98
Lloyd George, David 94, 122
Longhurst, Henry 58
Lorimer, J. H. 84, 94

Macdonald, Charles Blair 74
Macfie, A. C. 72
McKellar, Alexander 124
McPherson, Rev. J. 62
Mallaby-Delley, H. 122
Mary Queen of Scots 58
Maxwell, Robert 122
Miller, T. H. 80
Minchinhampton Golf Club, Gloucestershire 60
Molesworth, Arthur 50, 64
Molesworth, Captain – 50, 56
Morris, (Old) Tom 44, 46, 48, 50, 62, 72, 86, 116
Morris, (Young) Tom 50, 116
Morrison, R. E. 76
Muirfield
    see Honourable Company of Edinburgh
    Golfers
Murray, Clive, engraver 62
Musselburgh 28, 34, 38, 46

National Gallery, London 10
Neer, van der 10
Neiman, LeRoy 114
Nicholson, F. 18
Nicklaus, Jack 114
North Berwick 30, 98

Oliphant, Robert 30
Orpen, Sir William 96
Ostade, van 10

Park, Willie, junior 46, 62
Park, Willie, senior 46, 62, 116
Pau Golf Club 70
Pearson, Issette 66, 80
Pebble Beach 114
Pimm, William E. 64
'Pipeshank, George' 124
Playfair, Major – 36
Prestwick, 44, 46
Professional Golfers Association/World Golf Hall
    of Fame (USA) 82
Prosperi, Liberio see 'Lib'
Purves, Dr W. Laidlaw 64, 66, 68

Raeburn, Sir Henry 9, 28, 38
Ramsbottam, A. M. 86
Reed, Kenneth 118
Reid, Sir George 86
Reid, John 74
Rembrandt 12
Reynolds, Frank 124
Riddell, Lord 94
Robertson, Allan 38, 40, 44, 48
Robertson, C. H. 34
Rountree, Harry 124
Royal and Ancient Golf Club 7, 10, 16, 36, 38, 40,
    42, 44, 46, 48, 72, 84, 86, 88, 90, 92, 96, 104, 120
Royal Blackheath Golf Club (or Blackheath) 20,
    26, 28, 30, 32, 34, 46, 48, 52, 56, 66
Royal Burgess Society of Edinburgh 22, 34, 38
Royal Company of Archers, Edinburgh 22
Royal Liverpool Golf Club (inc. Hoylake) 54, 56,
    76, 88, 102
Royal North Devon Golf Club (inc. Westward Ho!)
    54, 56, 58
Royal St George's Golf Club, Sandwich 54, 66, 68
Royal West Norfolk Golf Club 110
Royal Wimbledon Golf Club 54, 64, 66

Sadler, W. Dendy 92
St Andrews 7, 16, 36, 40, 42, 48, 50, 58, 62, 72, 90, 120
St Andrew's Golf Club, USA 74
St Clair, William 22, 28
Sandy, Paul 18
Sayers, Ben 78
Scott, Lady Margaret 60
Scottish National Portrait Gallery 24, 36
Sealy, Allen C. 68, 70
Sharpe, Corporal Archibald 32
Smart, John 98
Spencelayh, Charles 68
'Spy' (Sir Leslie Ward), 88, 122
Stevenson, W. G. 62
Stewart, Captain 54
Stoddart, Laurence 74

Tait, Freddie 72, 78, 84
Taylor, J. H. 72, 90, 122
Taylor, John 28
Taylor, R., engraver 60
Turnberry, Ailsa Course 118

United States Golf Association 20, 74, 100, 108, 122

Vanity Fair 122
Vardon, Harry 90
Velde, Adriaen van de 10

Wagstaff, Charles E., engraver 36
Walker, J., engraver 18
Walton Heath 94
Ward, Sir Leslie see 'Spy'
Watson, James Fletcher 110
Watson, Tom 114
Weaver, Arthur 86, 122, 116
Westward Ho! see Royal North Devon Golf Club
Whyte-Melville, John 30, 42
Wills, J. Anthony 108
Wimbledon Common 64
Wood, Lawson 124